"This book is an excellent guide for school leaders who want to move beyond management and become true instructional leaders. Joe and T.J. provide clear, actionable tools that help school administrators give feedback while also building a culture where guidance fuels growth. This book blends the reality of leading schools with the importance of shaping instruction. *Time, Tools, and Tactics of Instructional Leadership* is practical, relevant, and inspiring."
Todd Whitaker, *Author and Speaker*

"When readers see themselves in the stories of the book, you know the authors have accomplished something special. That is what you have with *Time, Tools, and Tactics of Instructional Leadership: A Principal's Guide to Leading Learning* by Joe Jones and T.J. Vari. It is an immensely practical road map for any school leader hoping to move the needle with student achievement. With actionable items in every chapter, it becomes an immediate new tool for every educator looking to strengthen their toolbox."
Danny Steele, *Author, Speaker, and Former Principal*

"*Time, Tools, and Tactics of Instructional Leadership* is exactly what school leaders need right now. Dr. Jones and Dr. Vari provide practical strategies that help principals move from managing the urgent to leading the important. This book is more than theory—it's a step-by-step guide for getting into classrooms, giving meaningful feedback, and building systems that truly impact teaching and learning. As a principal and national education leader, I know this resource will inspire and equip administrators to lead with clarity and confidence."
Evelyn Edney, *Principal, Early College High School at Delaware State University; President, NASSP*

"The book *Times, Tools, and Tactics of Instructional Leadership: A Principal's Guide to Leading Learning* is an excellent resource for school leaders focused on improving the quality of instruction in their schools, developing the talent of their staff, and creating a climate focused on teaching and learning rather than crisis management."
From the Foreword by **Jackie Owens Wilson,** *Executive Director, National Policy Board for Educational Administration, USA*

"*Time, Tools, and Tactics of Instructional Leadership: A Principal's Guide to Leading Learning* is an essential read for current and future school leaders. In it, experienced education leaders and authors, Dr. Vari and Dr. Jones, argue that true school leadership is rooted in instructional leadership. While principals and assistant principals often feel too overwhelmed to regularly visit classrooms, the authors emphasize that these visits are what make the role most meaningful. Using their "3T Method"—time, tools, and tactics—they offer a practical roadmap to help leaders shift their focus, manage their responsibilities, and effectively guide teachers and staff toward stronger instruction."

Mitch Weathers, *CEO, Organized Binder*

"As someone who has worked alongside countless principals, instructional coaches, and leaders, I see the same story repeated over and over again: they're overwhelmed, exhausted, and stretched in every direction, constantly putting out fires. This book is the lightbulb moment they've all been waiting for. It breaks things down with such clarity and precision that it both affirms what we know to be true, and offers the practical path forward that leaders have been searching for. For every educator in a leadership position, this isn't just a powerful read—it's essential."

Kim Gameroz, *Founder and CEO of Teaching Inside Out*

"Timely, Relevant, and Needed! Principals and school leaders will find this essential guide packed with research-backed strategies, real-world examples, and practical techniques. Timely topics such as instructional leadership, effective feedback, and managing change among others are included in this much needed guide. Whether for professional development or personal growth, this book is relevant and a must-read for anyone ready to lead with lasting impact."

Sharon Pepukayi, *Superintendent*

"This book is a masterful roadmap for instructional leaders seeking clarity, practical strategies, and impactful results in school leadership. With actionable time management tools, research-driven tactics, and a clear framework for guiding professional growth, Joe and T.J. have created an essential resource for principals determined to elevate learning for every student and staff member. Their experience shines through on every page, offering inspiration and concrete steps for leading learning with purpose and effectiveness."

Joshua Stamper, *Keynote Speaker and Author*

Time, Tools, and Tactics of Instructional Leadership

Let's face it, many school leaders are trapped in operation and management mode—this book will get you unstuck! Expert authors Jones and Vari provide a practical and empowering guide to help school leaders reclaim their time and sharpen their focus on improving teaching and learning. Based on the 3Ts method—time, tools, and tactics—this book helps principals and assistant principals become more intentional and impactful instructional leaders.

Each chapter offers actionable strategies and tactics that guide leaders toward spending more time in classrooms offering feedback and less time managing crises that others are better equipped to handle. By differentiating urgent from important work, offering a clear roadmap for leadership growth, and unpacking effective feedback practices to ensure the leader's message is highly impactful, this book helps leaders lift not only their own performance but also the entire school community. Whether you're new to your role, an aspiring leader, seasoned administrator, or a district-level coach, this book delivers the clarity and structure needed to lead instruction with confidence and purpose. Everyone knows the importance of instructional leadership; this book is designed to help leaders learn the skills to do it well!

Joseph Jones is the superintendent of New Castle County Vocational and Technical School District in Delaware, USA. He is co-founder of the leadership development institute, TheSchoolhouse302.

T.J. Vari is the Senior Director of Product Strategy at MaiaLearning. Vari is a former deputy superintendent, middle school assistant principal and principal, and high school English teacher. He is also co-founder of the leadership development institute, TheSchoolhouse302.

Also Available from Routledge Eye On Education
(www.routledge.com/eyeoneducation)

Emotionally Intelligent School Leadership: Lead with Heart, Transform with Purpose
Brandy L. Tackett

A Guide to Early College and Dual Enrollment Programs: Designing and Implementing Programs for Student Achievement, 2nd Edition
Russell Olwell

School Change is a Collaborative Process: A Step-by-Step Guide to Improve K-12 Student Learning
Stephen Gould

Where the Science of Improvement Meets the Heart of Leadership: Leading Equity-Focused School and District Improvement
Marci Shepard

K-12 Schools and Public Health Partnerships: Strategies for Navigating a Crisis with Trust, Equity, and Communication
Leah Perkinson, Lisa C. Barrios, Rebecca Lee Smith, Rachel Roegman

A Blueprint for Teacher Retention: Leading Schools that Teachers Don't Want to Leave
James A. Bailey

Your School Leadership Edit: A Minimalist Approach to Rethinking Your School Ecosystem
Tamera Musiowsky-Borneman, C.Y. Arnold

Game-Changing Leadership in Action: An Educator's Companion
Kim Wallace

Time, Tools, and Tactics of Instructional Leadership

A Principal's Guide to Leading Learning

Joseph Jones and T.J. Vari

Designed cover image: © Getty Images

First published 2026
by Routledge
605 Third Avenue, New York, NY 10158

and by Routledge
4 Park Square, Milton Park, Abingdon, Oxon, OX14 4RN

Routledge is an imprint of the Taylor & Francis Group, an informa business

© 2026 Joseph Jones and T.J. Vari

The right of Joseph Jones and T.J. Vari to be identified as authors of this work has been asserted in accordance with sections 77 and 78 of the Copyright, Designs and Patents Act 1988.

All rights reserved. No part of this book may be reprinted or reproduced or utilised in any form or by any electronic, mechanical, or other means, now known or hereafter invented, including photocopying and recording, or in any information storage or retrieval system, without permission in writing from the publishers.

For Product Safety Concerns and Information please contact our EU representative GPSR@taylorandfrancis.com. Taylor & Francis Verlag GmbH, Kaufingerstraße 24, 80331 München, Germany.

Trademark notice: Product or corporate names may be trademarks or registered trademarks, and are used only for identification and explanation without intent to infringe.

ISBN: 978-1-041-20030-7 (hbk)
ISBN: 978-1-041-20029-1 (pbk)
ISBN: 978-1-003-71473-6 (ebk)

DOI: 10.4324/9781003714736

Typeset in Warnock
By codeMantra

Contents

Meet the Authors   *xiii*
Foreword by Jackie Owens Wilson   *xv*
Preface   *xix*

▶ **Part 1:**
The Core of Instructional Leadership   **1**

1. Introduction—Becoming an Instructional Leader   3
2. Finding the Time   15
3. Knowing What to Look For   29

▶ **Part 2:**
Effective and Meaningful Feedback   **43**

4. Celebrating Teachers   45
5. Making Incremental Progress   61
6. Improving Conversations   77

▶ **Part 3:**
Systems for Managing Change   **95**

7. Anchoring, Focusing, and Aligning the Work   97
8. Dealing with Resistance   113
9. Conclusion—Fostering Continuous Improvement   131

Meet the Authors

▶ **Joseph Jones** is the superintendent of New Castle County Vocational and Technical School District. Starting his career as a social studies teacher, he rose to the principalship at Delcastle Technical High School, earning Delaware's Outstanding Academic Achievement Award and Secondary Principal of the Year. He holds a doctorate in educational leadership from the University of Delaware and co-founded TheSchoolHouse302, a leadership development institute with an international footprint. Jones is a recognized speaker and co-author of seven books on educational leadership.

▶ **T.J. Vari** is the Senior Director of Product Strategy at MaiaLearning, with a focus on postsecondary planning for students worldwide. Vari is a former deputy superintendent, middle school assistant principal and principal, and high school English teacher. Vari is an award-winning educator, recognized speaker, and the co-founder of TheSchoolHouse302, a leadership development company with an international footprint. He is the co-author of seven books on educational leadership, which are the basis for his speaking engagements, coaching, and leadership development institutes.

Foreword

As school leaders we tend to be fixers. When someone on our staff comes to us, we want to immediately solve the problem so that the problem goes away and the staff member is happy. The problem with this is that our quick fixes may not resolve the underlying issues that created the problem, and it is often a temporary solution to a bigger issue. The other problem is that we often allow these requests to interrupt our day and keep us from focusing on the important work of leading instruction in the school or district. In the book *Time, Tools, and Tactics of Instructional Leadership: A Principal's Guide to Leading Learning*, authors Joseph Jones and T.J. Vari define the differences between urgent and important work and introduce us to the 3Ts method—time, tools, and tactics. The practices are aimed at helping school leaders learn more about themselves and the environment where they lead in order to improve instruction and provide greater opportunities for students.

Joseph Jones and T.J. Vari have spent years as instructional leaders in various schools and districts. They have also provided professional learning and coaching to hundreds of school leaders. They have tested the strategies they recommend with principals, assistant principals, and teacher leaders. They understand that the work we ask school leaders to do is complex and often time sensitive. They also know that schools are filled with daily distractions that often derail and take the leader away from the most important work, which is getting into classrooms where they observe and provide feedback to teachers about the quality of instruction provided to students. They have shared many of these lessons in their other books such as *Invest in Your Best, Passionate Leadership, 7 Mindshifts for School Leaders, Retention for Change, Building a Winning Team,* and *Candid and Compassionate Feedback*.

A central message of this book is defining urgent versus important work. The authors provide examples and questions to help the school leader determine what is urgent work versus important work. They go a step further by asking the school leader to determine if the problem needs to be solved by them or if the problem is something that someone else can resolve. They provide tools to guide the school leader in how to determine urgent problems that need to be solved right away and urgent problems that need to be solved by me or someone else. Throughout this book, the authors remind the school leader that they must remain focused on instruction. Jones and Vari define what they mean by the core of instructional leadership, which is the school leader's ability to manage time so that they can spend it in the most important spaces of the school—the classroom. They also provide a guide for how to develop an instructional framework for classroom look-fors.

In the second part of this book, Joseph Jones and T.J. Vari provide models for communication and feedback that are evidence-based and tested models. They remind the reader about the importance of celebrating success with the staff and how to use a model of coaching to enhance their professional practice. They also provide guidance on how to use questioning to facilitate a discussion following an observation to build trust and rapport with the teacher in order to improve instruction.

The authors also explore the school system including the vision, professional learning opportunities, and school improvement strategies. Sometimes the problems that emerge in schools are systems issues that need to be resolved in order to move forward with the important work of instruction. Jones and Vari discuss this and how to identify and resolve those issues. They also provide a model for supporting staff that may be resistant to the necessary changes that the school leader must make to address systems issues.

The book *Times, Tools, and Tactics of Instructional Leadership: A Principal's Guide to Leading Learning* is an excellent resource for school leaders focused on improving the quality of instruction in their schools, developing the talent of their staff, and creating a climate focused on teaching and learning rather than crisis management. As you engage with this book, consider how you can become more focused on instructional leadership by determining what is urgent and important work. The most important work we do as school leaders is to create an environment focused on the teaching and learning of students, staff, and our communities. This book is a great resource to help us accomplish that goal.

Jackie Owens Wilson, Ed.D.
Executive Director
National Policy Board for Educational Administration

Preface

This book is an answer to the constant tug of war that administrators face each day—the tension between dealing with the urgent issues and spending time in the work that truly makes a difference for our staff and students. Like many of you who picked up this book, we envisioned spending our days in classrooms, coaching teachers, studying data, and influencing curriculum, all with the goal of improving learning outcomes for our students. Yet, the average day of an administrator can actually have nothing to do with instruction. The bombardment of emails, daily emergencies, and countless meetings can eclipse most well-intentioned days. Operations can easily trump teaching and learning.

That's why we wrote this book—to help school leaders reclaim their time, sharpen their focus, and execute each day with precision. *Time, Tools, and Tactics of Instructional Leadership* offers a framework for becoming the kind of leader who you know your school needs and deserves. Our focus throughout this book is to provide clear ways that you can be the lead learner in your school and district.

▶ WHY THIS BOOK

We've had the good fortune to lead schools and districts successfully, coach administrators across the nation, and connect with leaders at all levels to know that being an instructional leader requires constant attention and intention. Most administrators truly desire to be instructional powerhouses in their schools but lack the specific skills needed to do so. The problem is that it isn't a matter of passion and will to be a lead learner; rather, it's a mindset backed by a strong skill set that enables administrators to stay in the important work. We find that the real challenge isn't knowing what to do; it's finding the time and the systems to do it consistently.

That's why this book focuses on the 3Ts—time, tools, and tactics—practical levers that equip leaders to lead with impact.

Each element is grounded in research, tested in schools, and refined over the years. Our practices for "time" usage are meant for you to manage yourself and your day to begin to live your vision as a lead learner, our "tools" are meant for you to employ a model or method that works to solve a problem, and our "tactics" are used to influence others.

This book is not a one-size-fits-all approach to school transformation. Instead, it's intended to keep you, the leader, at the center of school improvement. It gives you frameworks and methods that can be tailored to your school's culture, your team's capacity, and your own leadership style. Our goal is for you to finish this book not just inspired, but equipped with specific skills that can be implemented immediately.

▶ ORGANIZATION OF THIS BOOK

This book has three parts, each designed to build upon the last in a progressive development of stackable skills that progress from understanding and awareness to practice and mastery.

> *Part 1: The Core of Instructional Leadership* begins with reclaiming your time and allocating it in accordance with your vision to be the lead learner in your school. The *Introduction* sets the stage by connecting you with your purpose as an instructional leader and clearly distinguishing the urgent work from the important work.
> - *Chapter 2: Finding the Time* introduces two key ideas that allow school leaders to thrive—time blocking and reverse time blocking—two simple yet transformative strategies to make your instructional leadership work clearly visible in your calendar.
> - *Chapter 3: Knowing What to Look For* subtly shifts the focus from *when* you lead to *how* you lead. This chapter defines clear *Principles of Instruction* and uses them to anchor your classroom visits with meaningful feedback.
>
> *Part 2: Effective and Meaningful Feedback* moves from personal systems to interpersonal influence. Feedback is the vehicle through which leaders change instruction, and

this section provides three models that redefine how feedback works effectively in schools.
- *Chapter 4: Celebrating Teachers* unpacks the neuroscience of praise and demonstrates how "Specific Praise" can reinforce excellence and effort, helping teachers to feel pride in their work.
- *Chapter 5: Making Incremental Progress* introduces "Performance Coaching," a model for driving small, consistent changes that build momentum over time.
- *Chapter 6: Improving Conversations* reframes professional dialogue by teaching leaders how to ask better questions, building a culture of trust, and creating reflective partnerships through thoughtful discourse instead of compliance-based conversations.

Part 3: Systems for Managing Change integrates everything you've learned throughout this book into a systematic schoolwide approach to better teaching and learning.
- *Chapter 7: Anchoring, Focusing, and Aligning the Work* offers the A.F.A. model—a strategy for keeping your vision, incremental progress, and professional learning coherent rather than disjointed.
- *Chapter 8: Dealing with Resistance* introduces the IDEAS model to equip leaders to effectively manage resistance in a way that builds, rather than breaks relationships.
- The *Conclusion* closes with a call to action: a shift from a *teaching culture* to a *learning culture* through the Pressure-Support Model of Continuous Improvement. This is a leadership method for sustaining growth by balancing accountability with support and empathy.

Each part of this book is practical, with each skill set building off the other by design. You'll find a familiar character who is struggling in one or more areas of instructional leadership, models to support you as the lead learner, sample language to use, and next steps that can be executed tomorrow. Every concept has been field tested in schools and refined through coaching hundreds of leaders at every level within schools and districts, from assistant principals to superintendents.

▶ INTENDED AUDIENCE

This book is written for school and district leaders who want to be highly effective instructional leaders. It's especially useful for assistant principals and principals who are tired of putting out endless fires, spending too much time in operations, and who truly want to move from just supervising instruction to actually leading it. This book is also a powerful resource for aspiring administrators, instructional coaches, leadership teams, and principal supervisors. Anyone who can or wants to influence instruction should read this book.

While rooted in K–12 education, the 3Ts framework—time, tools, and tactics—applies broadly to any leadership role where people, purpose, and performance require effective communication. The lessons throughout this book are as relevant to central office directors as they are to teacher leaders who aspire to greatness in the classroom.

▶ SPECIAL FEATURES

To make this book both reflective and actionable, we've included:

- Frameworks and Models: Practical, repeatable systems like Specific Praise, Performance Coaching, A.F.A., and IDEAS that can be implemented immediately.
- Next Step Checklists: Prompts that help leaders translate ideas into action, either individually or in team discussions.
- Field-Tested Strategies: Each chapter includes a sample scenario drawn from real situations and a *time* strategy, a specific *tool*, or a *tactic* for implementation. Names of schools and individuals were changed to protect anonymity.
- Consistent Thread of Application: Every section connects back to the central question—*How does this improve teaching and learning in my school?*

▶ A FINAL THOUGHT

If you've ever sat at your desk at the end of the day wondering where the time went, wished you would have spent more time in classrooms, or engaged in better conversations with teachers on instruction, then this book is for you. Please know that *Time, Tools, and Tactics of Instructional Leadership* isn't about you doing more and working longer hours. Rather, it's about working with intention every day with proven models to support you. It's about leading your school or district the way you envisioned you would when you first accepted the role.

Our hope is that you'll see yourself on every page, not as the overwhelmed administrator you might feel some days, but as the instructional leader you're becoming.

Part 1

The Core of Instructional Leadership

1 Introduction— Becoming an Instructional Leader

When assistant principals and principals think about what they want to accomplish as school leaders—whether it's their first year on the job or their tenth—they want to improve instruction and student outcomes. Even when asked about their general responsibilities as a supervisor, most will name instructional leadership as a key responsibility of the role. And, unfortunately, many school leaders struggle to be effective instructional leaders regardless of their desire to be one.

If you're reading this book, you want to be a more effective instructional leader. Whether you're an aspiring administrator, a current school leader, an instructional coach, a teacher leader, or a district office administrator who supports instructional leaders, if your goal is to get into more classrooms to help teachers to be their best, we applaud you. If you're haunted by the worry that you're not doing a good enough job with it, you're not alone. We've found through our school leader coaching methods—1:1 coaching, masterminds, executive coaching, and more—that there are more school leaders who are not doing what they wish to be doing with instructional leadership than there are leaders who are content with their efforts regarding instructional leadership.

When we wrote *7 Mindshifts for School Leaders* (Hamilton et al., 2022)—a book about solving persistent problems in schools—we identified that many leaders focus on urgent work instead of important work despite their desire to do so. Although that book is about strategies for problem-solving rather than a pure instructional leadership book, we uncovered the reality that too many leaders are stuck on urgent versus important problems. One of those problems, which we address in *this* book, is that leaders lack the necessary strategies that we refer to as *time, tools, and tactics* (the 3Ts) of instructional leadership. In other words, school leaders who find themselves mired in urgent work, longing to be more effective instructional leaders, don't always know how to carve out the *time*, lack the necessary *tools*, and aren't equipped with the *tactics* to execute effectively. The 3Ts provide a clear method for leaders to employ so that as their day unfolds and the urgent issues rise, they are empowered to handle them without sacrificing the important work that truly moves the needle of teacher effectiveness and student achievement.

▶ URGENT VERSUS IMPORTANT WORK

In working with principal supervisors, superintendents, and other district staff who oversee principals and assistant principals, we often find what appears to be a lack of clarity about the difference between urgent and important work. However, it's rarely the case that the school leaders are actually confused about what's urgent versus important. As we dig deeper into their management philosophies, we find that "confusion" lies with *who* should be putting out the urgent fires that pop up throughout the day and *when* some of these issues need to be tackled. It's not that the school leaders believe that they should be mired in urgent work, unable to get to the important stuff, it's that they don't have systems for making the distinction between who should do what and in which order.

Most school leaders are natural problem solvers who are grounded in altruism. Educators want to help students and, in turn, impact the community and even the world. It's refreshing to work with people who have an innate desire to make a difference for students, their families, and the communities in which we live. It's ironic that such a noble quality can also be an Achilles heel when making day-to-day decisions about where to place our focus.

The reality is that schools are complex with nonstop operational and managerial hurdles. Sometimes it feels like nothing can go right. The air conditioning isn't functioning. The cafeteria didn't get cleaned after last night's event. A parent is demanding to see the principal in the main office. A bus driver hit a parked car in a neighborhood. A third grade student has a pocket knife in his backpack. The physics teacher went into labor during the school day. It's constant, endless, and all at once. There is no question that any school leader can simply show up to work without anything on their calendar and be swamped all day, solving problems that they never expected.

The challenge with each of the complications listed above is that they aren't the school leader's problems to solve, but they do it anyway. There are three primary reasons why school leaders behave this way:

1. There's an emotionally gratifying effect of solving a problem for someone else. A problem pops up, the leader solves it. Pretty soon, they become so good at solving urgent and unexpected problems that everyone brings their problems to them and expects them to take care of them right away. It can even feel so good to lead this way that we don't even evaluate whether or not it's effective. On our best day, we solve all the problems that come our way. On our worst day, there ends up being too many problems to solve, leaving a few on our to-do list for tomorrow.
2. Some school leaders operate under the unhealthy belief that they're the arbiter of all efforts to maintain a positive school culture and climate. They take it on as solely their responsibility even though a positive culture and climate are the result of a collective effort, not a single person's work. This creates a fear-based decision-making model because they need to be included in every decision that gets made due to anxiety about what happens if the wrong decision prevails. Not only does this slow down progress for the school, but it also creates a scenario where the leader is bogged down by urgent and sometimes mundane work.
3. Lastly, school leaders get stuck in urgent work when they're always in crisis-management mode. They might not be

gratified by the urgent work, but their brain responds to most tasks as if it was a crisis that needed to be prevented. Everything is seen through the lens of a worst-case scenario. And, not everything ends up worst-case, which means that the time and energy put into worst-case thinking and worst-case planning is wasted rather than being spent on important work.

Let's turn to Table 1.1, which illustrates the difference between urgent and important work and *who* should be responsible for each. It's interesting that many school leaders spend most of their time operating in quadrants 1 and 2. The obvious goal is to spend most of your time in quadrant 4, and quadrant 3 should be rare. In fact, if quadrant 3 is a persistent problem, your school has bigger issues that need your attention before instructional leadership should become your priority. That's not the case in most schools, though.

Let's unpack quadrants 1 and 2, where most school leaders spend their time. Quadrant 1 is the result of the three missteps described above. The problems present themselves, and you solve them, becoming great at solving minute-to-minute problems and making decisions for people who ultimately become dependent on you to make every decision for them. Quadrant 2 illuminates a different issue where a leader is either micromanaging the tasks that they should expect others to do or hasn't distributed leadership properly so that others are empowered to solve problems on their own. These are both quadrants to avoid at all costs.

In any event, you can't lead a school and improve instruction if you're caught in quadrants 1–3 all the time. To become

Table 1.1 Urgent versus Important Work

	Urgent	Important
Me	Q3 A crisis that only I can handle as the leader	Q4 The vision I have for how my day should unfold
Not Me	Q1 Most problems that arise during a given school day	Q2 Tasks that are assigned to other leaders in the school

an instructional leader, you must spend the vast majority of your time in quadrant 4 with a vision for engaging in high-leverage instructional leadership activities, such as being in classrooms conducting walkthroughs and observations, engaging with teachers in professional learning communities (PLCs) where you can provide targeted feedback, discussing and evaluating relevant data, having one-on-one coaching and support sessions with teachers, and building a culture of learning.

We find that school leaders know this to be true, but don't necessarily know how to shift their current conditions to be able to make the important work the prevalent work. We honor the fact that schools are complex organizations where problems do arise in quadrant 3, which require a response from an assistant principal or principal, but we also know that school leaders need the *time, tools, and tactics* (3Ts) to build a day that ensures a strong focus on instructional leadership.

▶ THE 3TS METHOD

In each chapter of this book, you'll find a practice that falls in one of three categories—*time, tools,* and *tactics.* All of the practices are aimed at helping school leaders to learn about themselves and their environment to lift student achievement to new heights. This book is designed to teach you how to be an instructional leader and give you all of what you need to do so effectively. Before we get to our first tool—Asking Two Questions—we want to provide a brief description of what we're trying to accomplish with the 3Ts.

▶ Dedicating Time

Our practices for "time" usage are meant for you to dedicate time in specific blocks and then reflect on your day and evaluate how your time is being used or misused. You'll find practices for saving and using time in Chapters 2 and 8 and Conclusion. We start and end with *time* on purpose because it's the only way that you can begin to think about how to use your time as an instructional leader and then employ everything that you're going to learn in this book.

▶ Using Tools

Our "tools" are meant for you to employ a model or method that works to solve a problem that you're experiencing and won't likely be solved without a tool. Tools are directed *at you* versus tactics, which we direct *toward others*. Tools range from a specific set of questions to ask yourself to things that you should look for in every classroom to the way that you should frame your feedback to teachers. Tools appear in Introduction and Chapters 3 and 7.

▶ Employing Tactics

Our "tactics" are used to influence others. As John Maxwell says, "leadership is influence—nothing more, nothing less" (Maxwell, 1998). The tactics are the heart of the book and the backbone of your leadership when it comes to improving instruction. They appear in Chapters 4–6. Because these tactics are public, meaning your teachers will hear, read, and feel their effects, you should practice them as much as you can.

▶ THE TOOL: ASKING TWO QUESTIONS

Let's unpack our first tool. When we coach school leaders, many of whom are bogged down by urgent versus important work, we tell them to ask themselves two questions whenever they're on their way to do important work and an urgent matter seems to divert their attention.

> **Question Number One:** *Does this "urgent" problem need to be solved right now?*
> **Question Number Two:** *Does this "urgent" problem need to be solved by me?*

For assistant principals and principals who are constantly interrupted during the school day, the answer to these questions is invariably "no" and "no." Most of the time, problems that have naturally arisen during the school day—unpredictable issues—are not problems that need to be solved immediately. And, even when they do need an emergent solution, they likely don't need the attention of an assistant principal or a principal. We can tell you from experience that there's a kitchen manager, chief custodian, school nurse, counselor, administrative assistant, or teacher leader who is equipped to address the issue at hand and, in many cases, is better suited to solve the problem than the school principal.

As far as the tool goes, we literally recommend that school leaders write these two questions down on a 3X5 card and carry the card around in their pocket, taking the card out for use whenever something unplanned comes up. It's just too easy to forget to use the questions or to forget what the questions are in the moment-to-moment chaos of the school day. Having the questions written and available makes the tool much easier to use, and tools are only as effective as the frequency in which they're used. Let's unpack the questions a bit further.

▶ Question Number One: Does This "Urgent" Problem Need to Be Solved Right Now?

The truth about Question Number One is that the problem might actually just be easiest to solve right then so that the task is complete. Sometimes the convenience of solving the problem seems as feasible as making it wait. All that ever does is to delay the other work that you intended to do. The *easiest* thing to do—solve the problem—is not always the *right* thing to do. If the problem can wait, it should, which allows you to continue on with your predetermined plan, which should be a high-leverage instructional leadership activity.

We also find, through our own experience and our work with school leaders, that these "urgent" problems are almost never associated with student learning. They're typically operational regarding a broken elevator, the arrival of the bookstore materials, or an angry parent on the other end of the phone. None of these examples require you to change the course of your day, especially if it means skipping the work you planned to do as an instructional leader.

▶ Question Number Two: Does This "Urgent" Problem Need to Be Solved by Me?

As described above, the reality of Question Number Two is that it could be gratifying to help the person who brings the problem to you, and in doing so you might be robbing that satisfaction from someone else. As a busy school leader, it's far better to be a conduit for problem-solving than to constantly solve all the problems. Asking whether or not you're the right person to solve the problem also implies that you should know who else is capable. You can't actually control the culture and climate yourself, and not everything is a crisis that you need to handle. When the "urgent" problem gets to you, think of it as a teachable moment—for both you and the person who emerged with the issue. You're learning to let go; they're learning to find the right person on the team.

This means that you're reflecting on your staff as problem solvers, rolling through your mental rolodex to pinpoint who the problem should be routed to. When you name that person for the individual who brought you the problem, you're teaching them that these kinds of issues don't need to come directly to you and that you're not going to solve every problem as the leader. In fact, once the school leader embraces and accepts that their day must live in quadrant 4, they begin to communicate to their staff about their philosophy and how they intend to structure their day.

Leaders don't want to inadvertently send a message that they don't care or that certain work is beneath them, but rather express who is responsible for what and why and how that ultimately benefits everyone. This approach reinforces that the school is a community and that you are a focused school leader who is determined to effectively lead it.

▶ FOCUSED SCHOOL LEADERSHIP

This book is broken into three parts to keep you focused as a school leader. Without focus, it's not possible to be an instructional powerhouse. In the first part, we reveal the core of instructional leadership, which is your ability to manage time so that you can spend it in the most important spaces in your school—the classroom. And we provide a guide for how to develop an instructional framework so that your look-fors are crystal clear.

In the second part, we reveal three research-based and field-tested models for communication and feedback. The first is about celebrating the work of your staff. The second is a model for coaching to enhance practice. The third is a questioning technique that breaks the mold of what you typically understand about how to use questions after an observation, and it's far more effective at building relationships and managing change.

The third part dives into systems, including how to reinforce the school vision, support professional development, and make incremental progress toward massive improvements. We also unveil a model for what to do when teachers are either reluctant to change or simply dig their heels in against it. We believe that every administrator needs to know all of the models in this book to lead instruction effectively.

Finally, there are three other aspects of the book that you should be aware of. The first is that each chapter starts with a common story about a school leader who needs help. Woven through the stories is a consistent character with the nickname, Yoda. Yoda is a former highly effective school leader who coaches each of the characters in the stories to become stronger leaders in the realm of managing their school and taking proven steps to improve the quality of the instruction in every classroom. Second, each chapter has a "Leader Well-Being Side Note" to ensure that your mind and body are healthy. You can't pour from an empty cup. Third, every chapter ends with a "Next Steps Checklist" so that you can get started implementing right away.

▶ Part 1: The Core of Instructional Leadership

To be an instructional leader, you have to be where the instruction takes place. Leaders should find themselves spending their time in the most important spaces in their organization; for school leaders, that's the classroom. We can't stress that enough, and we'll repeat it throughout the book. We begin with your use of time because that's the only way to become a true instructional leader. All of Chapter 2 is dedicated to how you use the time you have during the school day. Chapter 3 is about learning to use an instructional framework, called *Principles of Instruction*, something that we teach school leaders about in terms of understanding that there are teaching strategies that work better than others.

▶ Part 2: Effective and Meaningful Feedback

Chapter 4 is your first and most important form of feedback, which is the praise that you'll use to lift, celebrate, and support the work of your teachers. In Chapter 5, we discuss the need to make incremental adjustments and improvements to teachers' classroom environments to better support learning. And, Chapter 6 is about asking better questions to prompt your teachers as reflective practitioners, something you'll learn that they aren't likely to do on their own.

▶ Part 3: Systems for Managing Change

Chapter 7 is about anchoring, focusing, and aligning your feedback to professional development efforts, your school's vision, and incremental improvements over time. Chapter 8 and Conclusion drive home the cultural changes that you're seeking to make. In a "learning culture," everyone wants to grow, and feedback is at the center of that, but we know that there is often resistance, especially in the beginning. You're going to need strategies when the naysayers come forward. The leader is responsible for the culture, but making continuous improvement to practice is everyone's job. There's no place for complacency in a school where we're learning and lifting together.

▶ A Roadmap for the Reader or How This Book Is Written for You

It's important for you to know that this book is written in a linear fashion with precise steps to take toward being a master instructional leader. The hard truth is that you can't be an instructional leader if you aren't able to manage yourself and your time effectively, which is discussed in Introduction and

Chapter 2. Chapter 3 focuses on how it's critical that everyone knows what they're looking for when visiting classrooms. Chapter 4 introduces our first vital tactic, Specific Praise, which covers how celebrating teachers is the most important feedback tactic to elevate and reinforce best practices. Chapter 5 dives into incremental change through Performance Coaching, which is what leads to massive improvements in teacher performance and, consequently, student achievement. Chapter 6 covers the power of asking better questions through Professional Dialogue. Curiosity and conversations about our work lead to improved efforts and better results. Chapter 7 introduces our signature model, Anchor, Focus, and Align, A.F.A., which ensures that your feedback is meaningful and coherent and that your staff is motivated and energized about the work. Chapter 8 is focused on effectively influencing resistant teachers through a framework that you can use for having candid conversations and following up to observe the changes that are critical for them, their students, and the school culture. We conclude the book with a focus on creating a culture of continuous improvement that demands a balance of pressure and support.

Each one of the 3Ts builds on the previous in a way that creates your system for being an instructional leader. The design is intentionally progressive, like a staircase from novice to expert, ensuring that each step strengthens your foundation and prepares you for the next. We know that with the right *time, tools, and tactics*, you can lead learning the way that you intended when you set out on your journey to improve student outcomes for all kids.

References

Hamilton, C., Jones, J., & Vari, T. (2022). *7 mindshifts for school leaders: Finding new ways to think about old problems.* Thousand Oaks, CA: Corwin.

Maxwell, J. C. (1998). *The 21 irrefutable laws of leadership: Follow them and people will follow you.* Nashville, TN: Thomas Nelson.

Finding the Time

2

▶ MARA CAN'T FIND THE TIME

Mara was an excellent assistant principal for the past four years, and she just wrapped up her first full year as the principal of a middle school. Her time as AP was effective with a focus on instructional leadership, student support, and college and career exploration in a school that was top performing in the state. Now, in a neighboring district, she's the principal of a school with the need for some serious changes to old instructional practices that just aren't meeting the needs of the students. But, in her first year as principal, the only real instructional leadership she engaged in was a few professional learning sessions she held after school for the new teachers. As much as she wants to lead instruction, she just couldn't find the time to get into classrooms outside of her formal observation schedule. Mara needed a system.

At her performance appraisal that summer, Mara was praised for setting the tone and reestablishing the school vision. She admitted to her supervisor that she wanted to get into classrooms more often, but was struggling to find the time. They both agreed to allocate some of the Title II money from her school budget for a leadership coach. They searched online and found a number of available coaches, and Mara interviewed three and picked one that she thought was a fit based on his expertise with instructional leadership and administrative experience. In fact, his nickname is Yoda because of his ability to create other "Jedis." During their first meeting in July, the coach worked with Mara to set three big goals for the year, one of which was more informal classroom visits with feedback to teachers.

After Yoda read the goals, he asked Mara how she handled her day-to-day schedule. Yoda knew that goals are only as good as the strategies designed to support them. This led to a conversation about who managed her calendar and what strategies she used to ensure that her time was spent on the most effective practices for leading a school. Mara was at a loss. Her previous district had several systems in place that she now realized created the structure for much of her success as an AP. They were missing from this new role.

Despite having two main office secretaries, neither one was dedicated to Mara. She managed her own calendar, and she typically only blocked off time for teacher observations—which the experienced teachers set for themselves at the beginning of the school year. This meant that she had large swaths of time on her calendar that she intended to use for informal visits to classrooms, planning with teachers, and looking at data in professional learning communities (PLCs), but that wasn't happening.

Her time was being occupied by the minutiae of the day and the thousand small fires that occur in every school. Yoda told her that the first activity would be called "time blocking" and then she would learn to reverse-time-block. Mara was excited to get started.

▶ YOU'RE OUT OF TIME

Mara's time problems are common for many school leaders because managing time is really about managing yourself. And without systems in place, we succumb to the urgent and forgo the important. Schools are complex places, and school leaders can end up totally entrenched in "running the operations of the school" versus leading it. We find that leaders generally fall into one or more of the following three traps when it comes to not being able to realize the benefits of being an instructional leader.

▶ Trap #1: Getting Sidetracked by Operations and Management

The operational side of the school is as important as the instructional side. And, while instructional leadership can lead to fewer problems—engaging students helps to manage behaviors—it doesn't prevent the myriad of issues that inevitably arise. Any experienced principal can list the number of challenges that ensue on any given day that have nothing to do with quality instruction in the classroom. We'll come back to this issue later when we discuss the amount of time that leaders should spend on management versus instruction because your time is still going to be spent on management no matter what you do. The problem with the operational side is that it's endless—kids ride buses, they need to be fed, the bells ring and the hallways are full, recess and other communal spaces need supervision, the list goes on and on.

Operations and management are critical, and without a proper system in place, they can overshadow instructional leadership because it demands attention all the time. Schools need to be viewed as little cities, and if we're not careful with how we organize our time, instruction will naturally take a back seat. This happens because of two key factors:

1. Unlike the cafeteria or other pressing operational matters, instruction isn't physically visible or demanding immediate attention.
2. Instruction doesn't actively interrupt our day—teachers manage their classrooms independently, making it easy to assume instruction is running smoothly without direct oversight.

As a result, instructional leadership can become reactive rather than intentional. Prioritizing it requires a deliberate shift in the leader's focus.

This is also how silos are formed in schools. All of a sudden, every teacher is working in their own little school. Maybe they're collaborating, sharing resources and ideas, but what we typically find is that PLCs, and other collaborative efforts, suffer in sophistication and outcomes and can even fall off the map with each teacher working in isolation. Without regular visits to classrooms and cohesive structures for learning, the school becomes a place where administrators manage the operations and teachers work with students, receiving little feedback and stagnating growth.

▶ Trap #2: Believing that Your School Is Unique

Instructional leadership can be boiled down to how school leaders use their time. In *Invest in Your Best*, we used three identities—superstars, mediocres, and backbones—to represent teachers. The same idea applies to school leaders. Great school leaders, your superstars, are in classrooms for a large part of their day, backbones find it hard to get into classrooms, but do what is required and perhaps a little more, and mediocre school leaders can barely get their teacher observations done. The truth is that each administrator has the same amount of time in their school day as every other school leader, and schools, in general, are more alike than they are different.

Still, many school leaders fall into the trap of thinking that their school is so unique or different—their staff is unique, their student discipline is unique, their parents are unique, and so on—that it's impossible to spend time in classrooms or planning with teachers, but that's just not true. We don't want to suggest that there are not extreme challenges in some schools. However, we would argue that the more extreme the case, the more the need for instructional leadership.

We have to rid ourselves of any excuses for not being the instructional leader that our schools need and embrace the systems and strategies that yield success. If you're not getting into classrooms like you want, and you're telling yourself a story about how unique your school is as the reason why it's not happening, we ask you to reframe your thinking and start exploring the possibilities that we outline in this book.

▶ Trap #3: Focusing on Responsive Leadership

The third trap is that lots of school leaders have misconstrued what it means to be available. School leaders want to be responsive to the needs of the people in the school as well as the community at large. The issue is that leaders misunderstand what this means for their daily schedule. For example, leaders with "open door policies" and the availability to respond to emails in seconds flat might be creating a dysfunctional culture without knowing or intending to do so. Reacting to every situation, minute-by-minute, isn't what visionary leaders do. They stick to a plan (unless a real crisis emerges), and then execute the plan, keeping the main thing, the main thing. In schools, teaching and learning are the main things.

This doesn't mean that everyone needs to make an appointment to see the school leader when they have a quick question or that school leaders should have their door closed for large portions of the day to avoid what's going on. What it does mean is that leaders make specific time to be available and that they prioritize the time that they've allocated to be an instructional leader. The door should be closed and guarded for that matter, when you're conducting a pre- or post-observation conference. PLC time should be sacred, and a substantial block of each day should be allotted for informal classroom visits so that teachers can get ongoing feedback from assistant principals and principals.

▶ TAKING TIME TO MAKE TIME

It's important to take the time necessary to prepare for your day, week, month, and year. The only way to make time for what matters most is to carve out the time necessary to plan for how you intend to use your time. In this section, we're going to break down how you should *think* about time as an instructional leader, and in the next section, we're going to explain exactly *how* you can make your desired day a reality. Time management is both an art and a science. The art lies in the vision you create—the way you imagine using your time effectively. The science is in the reality of it, the choices you make, and how each minute and hour actually unfold.

The first thing to understand is that time is finite; we all get the same amount. The second thing to accept is that there's typically a huge gap between your intentions and your actions. You can intend to spend time in classrooms for 50 percent of your day and then get derailed all day long by minute-taker requests—students and staff who each need "one minute" of your time. "Do you have a minute?" is arguably the most frequently asked question of school leaders. The challenge is that it is never just one minute, and all of those minutes add up to equal your day. Your intentions are out the window. One of the major reasons that this happens to school leaders is when their day is open-ended and not carefully planned out. While it exists in their mind to visit classrooms, if those visits are not strategically planned and scheduled, they likely won't take place. Remember the mantra: *if it should be done, it must be planned, if it must be planned, it must be written down.*

Unplanned blocks of time are the enemy. They will almost always be consumed by the previously discussed traps—operations and management, your unique school needs, and responses to the minute-takers. The antidote is time-blocking—a strategy that we'll explain in detail in the next section. The other problem is that many leaders aren't grounded in reflection about what takes away all of their unplanned time. You were busy today, and we bet you can't even recall all of the things you did. That's normal and unfortunate. That's why we teach the skill of reverse-time-blocking (RTB) so that you have a smart way to review the time you spent on all of the aspects of your day that continue to prevent you from being the instructional leader you care to be.

▶ THE TIME: TIME-BLOCKING AND RTB

In the following three sections, we're going to unpack several strategies. In the first section, you're going to learn how to structure your day to be an instructional leader. It's the first step in the time equation to fitting all of the work of a school leader into one day without becoming distracted by all of the stuff happening around you. The second section is an explanation of how to block time on your calendar in a way that's intentional. The third section demonstrates how you can reverse-time-block and use your calendar as a reflection tool to solve problems and save time in the future. Note, though, that there are hidden gems within the sections that should not be overlooked, such as how you might use an assistant, vision work before the school year starts, and other aspects of developing your capacity to lead better.

▶ Time-Blocking

Your calendar is the key to your success. You either own it or someone else does. Yet, owning your calendar is not the same thing as managing it. Owning it means that you're operating with intention. Managing it can be done by someone else, as long as they understand your vision and goals for the day. If you are fortunate to have access to someone—an administrative assistant or secretary—who has the capacity to manage your calendar, then they should be managing your day. In other words, the only reason to manage your calendar is a lack of support staff who can assist. If you do have someone on staff who can manage your calendar, then you should set up a meeting with them after you read this chapter, have them read this section, and then work with them so that they can learn these strategies and use them to schedule your time.

The first strategy is called time-blocking. In general, it just means that your time is chunked into blocks and each block represents a task. The tasks can be meetings, events, classroom visits, observations, appointments, reminders, and any other aspect of life that is represented by time. Anything you spend time doing should be blocked on your calendar. It doesn't mean that every single second is blocked, we'll get to that with RTB. It does mean that all of your regularly scheduled tasks and monthly or yearly responsibilities are blocked on your calendar. For school leaders, especially those who want to be instructional leaders, it's best to do this in the summer when you can reflect on the previous year and plan for the future. If you're reading this in October, it's not too late, start time-blocking immediately, just don't block time for next week, though, do the remainder of the school year. We'll get to the granular details of this when we come back to Mara in a bit.

▶ Reverse-Time-Blocking

Some school leaders will be familiar with the concept of time-blocking, but we haven't met too many who are devoted to the proposition of RTB. RTB is a system for accounting for how you actually used your time. Time-blocking records how you intend to use your time; RTB chronicles what really happened.

As a school leader, you know that you can't totally and completely control how the day unfolds. A teacher could have an allergic reaction and need to go to the hospital, leaving a gap in coverage that you need to fill. Two students can have an altercation that seems to be spiraling on social media. As much as we want you to focus on important over urgent work, we know that any number of things can become real emergencies.

To use RTB, you simply capture whatever you ended up doing with your time in real-time. If you used all of your time the way it was blocked, then those blocks stay intact, and you RTB the open blocks so that every second is accounted for. If something changes because of an emergency or a quick decision you made during the day, then you change the blocked times to what truly occurred. The key is to use your calendar on your phone, tablet, or compute and reschedule what actually happened right after it happens (or shortly thereafter). At the end of every day and week, you want to have a complete picture of your interactions, who they were with, and why they transpired that way. This means that your calendar can be used as a reflection tool.

Cognitive scientists are clear that it's practically impossible to reflect on what you're doing while you're trying to do it. For us to ask you to reflect on your day or week to identify problems or to uncover bright spots would be an exercise in futility. When we ask school leaders why they're not getting into classrooms or attending PLCs, they always tell us that they're too busy. When we ask what they're busy doing, they usually say something like, "you know, all the stuff." Not only do we fail to reflect, the days get so far out in front of us that we fail to even remember all the things we did. What we definitely know is that there is too often more work than time. RBT is a great way to identify your primary time-takers. Now that you have your RTB calendar, you can look each day and each week at what you did. What we typically find is that a few parents, students, and teachers are the culprits for taking up a majority of your time. We find that there are recurring people and recurring problems. The RTB allows you to identify the things that are preventing you from achieving your daily goals and work to solve those problems proactively.

This is also why communicating to your staff and school community about your vision for how your day is designed is critical. We cannot assume that people know or appreciate what your day is like and what an instructional leader's high-leverage activities should be. After a few initial communications detailing how you schedule your day and why, you may need to have direct conversations with individuals as well. This can be as easy as telling a teacher that her fourth period plan is not the best time for you to be available for brainstorming. It might be that you need to design a process of how the behavior interventionist brings issues to you so that they don't hijack your day when they are completely capable of handling a group of students on their own. It could be as bold as telling a parent who always shows up unannounced that they'll need to make appointments in the future. Being clear to these individuals and your school community is imperative. You don't want to send the signal that you are never available or that you don't care. Rather, you want to establish healthy boundaries so that you can better serve your community.

The habit of an effective reverse time-blocking strategy doesn't just help to manage your time so that you can be a better instructional leader. It may also reveal critical insights into school-wide issues that you've been solving over-and-over with your time, unveiling the need for new systems. For the most part, you should be in charge of your day, not the other way around. Now that you understand time-blocking and RTB, let's see what it looks like in action during a given school day.

▶ The Day of an Instructional Leader

Most school leaders work 8–10 hours a day. We're not naive to the fact that some days are much longer than others, but our intent is to define the instructional school day. We realize, for a high school principal, a basketball game can mean a very late night, and school doesn't start late the next day just because you were there the previous day for 17 hours. The point here is that you have a specific period of time during the day where you're at work and the students aren't there yet or have left and the teachers aren't teaching. We're trying to manage three distinct parts of your day so that you can be an instructional leader—before students arrive, while students are in school and teachers are teaching, and after school hours.

Let's revisit Mara and her struggle with "finding time" to get into classrooms. She gets to work at 7AM, but the students don't arrive until 8:10AM. The students are dismissed each day at 2:55PM. The teachers' workday is 7.5 hours from 7:45AM to 3:15PM. The school day schedule is built on coverage, time requirements, and the teacher contract. It's like a puzzle. And, because it's a puzzle, so is your schedule each day. Mara's new coach has her start building her calendar in the summer. This is where having a vision for the school year—each month, each week, and each day—is critical.

From her coach's advice, Mara lists all of the things she must get done. She does bus duty each morning; not only does the bus lot need coverage, but she uses this time to make meaningful connections with students, looking for the smiles, greetings, and especially grunts or looks of sadness where she can intervene. This is a great opportunity for her to "see" her students and unofficially gauge their well-being. This means that from 7:55AM until 8:25AM, when the first bell rings, Mara is booked. Her coach instructs her to block that time on her calendar as a recurring item. We just allotted 30 minutes every day to bus coverage and student check-in. Since classes start at 8:25AM and end at 2:55PM, everyone is required to cover the dismissal, so Mara isn't so concerned about blocking time at the end of the day.

The coach is quick to point out that there are 2 times per month where Mara has to run a faculty meeting. Not only does she block off the faculty meeting times, she needs to prepare for the meetings, and she can't run a meeting that starts at 3PM by showing up at 3PM. She blocks the meetings and 20 minutes prior, and she blocks time in her calendar to plan for the meetings several weeks before they occur. This saves her 8–9 Sunday afternoons.

Next, all of the district meetings are blocked whereby Mara isn't even at school for a portion of the day. All of the teachers' PLC time is blocked so that Mara is keeping track of her meeting times. The lunch schedules are blocked. Mara covers A-lunch every day. All of the teachers she supervises need one or more observations based on their years of experience, and she takes the time to block them for the year. She knows that some of the teachers get to pick their observation schedule so she may have to change this later, but we need to see the time on her calendar that's left after everything is planned. She'll need to get the teachers to pick their observation times in the first few weeks of school so that her calendar can be adjusted accordingly.

Finally, after the must-do meetings and activities are scheduled, she can analyze the day to see where the high-leverage instructional leadership tasks should go. There are about 6 hours with students on any given day, and of the 6, about 4 of those hours are wide open. The coach knows Mara wants to visit classrooms informally through walkthroughs and learning walks, so she can gain insight on the level of instruction occurring and the consistency of curriculum implementation, in order to provide valuable feedback to her teachers. Mara wants to visit each of the teachers she supervises once a week, which is quite aggressive but doable if she plans well. She wants her assistant principal to do the same, but she needs to master the process first. The coach does the math, and that's about 4–6 visits per day, and because walkthroughs and learning walks are typically short visits at about 12–15 minutes, she needs approximately 90 minutes blocked per day for classroom visits.

In some cases, this is on top of an observation or postobservation, which means that Mara is spending about 2.5 hours a day as an instructional leader. This gives her almost 4 hours during the school day to manage everything else, and it gives her close to 7 hours of her typical work day to manage the school. Mara is actually surprised by how feasible this is, but she's been operating without a plan each day. Like a great deal of school leaders, she's filling her time with the hustle and bustle of the school and not her intentions to lead it.

There's one more valuable part to organizing these visits that the coach points out. Mara doesn't want to see each teacher on the same day each week or even the same time of day or even the same time of any given period of instruction. Mara has to spend a bunch of time ensuring that she gets to see each teacher on different days of the week each month and different times of the day for each visit. It takes her a while, but she maps it out. She even developed a coding system for herself so that she knows which times are the best on any given day within the time she blocked for informal visits. She has a nice swath of time each day that isn't planned, but she knows to use that for RTB and subsequent reflection, using that as a tool to solve recurring problems. And, she also knows that if the time that she planned for teacher visits gets eaten by something too urgent to ignore, she can flip the walkthrough schedule into the open time when that happens.

> **LEADER WELL-BEING SIDE NOTE: BALANCE—MANAGE YOURSELF, MANAGE YOUR TIME**
>
> If you're regularly working more than 10 hours a day, you might be your own worst enemy. Imposing that on yourself is cruel and unnecessary. We hope that time-blocking and reverse time-blocking can help. But, if your district normalizes 10+ hour days without regard for your well-being, then it may be time to find an organization that prioritizes balance over burnout.
>
> We've met too many school leaders who work 60, 70, and 80 hours a week with no end in sight while the neighboring district cares more about people than to let that happen. There are schools and districts that have created systems so that administrators aren't burning out and missing precious time with their families. Come back to the book after you find a new job or use the book for talking points in the interview you land for your next role.

▶ CONCLUSION

As Mara comes to understand, one of the most important and foundational aspects of becoming an instructional leader is to structure your time to accomplish the goals you set for classroom visits. Mara is going to make a huge leap from not doing very many visits to seeing each of her teachers every week. Of course, she'll hit potholes and pitfalls along the way, every school leader runs into obstacles, but she's setting herself up for success by time-blocking all of her intentions. She's also developing a mechanism to help her reflect on what happens when she's derailed.

By using RTB, she'll know exactly what happened and why, allowing her to make adjustments as needed. One last time-blocking tip, you can color-code your blocks to indicate the difference between operations and management and instructional leadership. This will give you one more tool to view your time and reflect on how you're using it. Use the Next Steps Checklist below to execute these strategies for yourself.

▶ Next Steps Checklist

- List all of your planned meetings, appointments, observations, and high-leverage instructional leadership activities for the school year (do this for the remainder of the school year if it has already started).
- Block out the appropriate amount of time for each of them.
- Decide how often you want to be in each classroom (every teacher in the school or just the ones you supervise).
- Block times for classroom walkthroughs and learning walks so that you have that time dedicated each day.
- Be sure to use RTB for anything that takes 5 or more of your minutes that you didn't pre-plan before it happened.
- Use your RTB at the end of each day and at the end of each week. Make note of recurring patterns in the things that are interrupting you. Develop systems to manage those patterns to create even more time for yourself.

3 Knowing What to Look For

▶ **DAVID'S TEACHERS ARE FRUSTRATED**

David is excellent at getting into classrooms. He uses the time-blocking and reverse-time-blocking strategies well, and he visits all of his teachers three times a month in accordance with his instructional leadership walkthrough goals. He's on track to reach his weekly, monthly, and yearly numbers that he set in July. But David isn't seeing the changes he would like, based on feedback that he leaves his teachers after each visit. And, the teachers are just as frustrated as David, and they have a really good reason.

David knows good instruction, and he's well-versed in effect sizes, cognitive science, and learning theory. The problem is that David's feedback is almost always completely random. He enters a classroom, observes for about 15 minutes, crafts feedback to the teacher, and sends it to them via email. This is all working well as a system. The concern that the teachers have is that the feedback is only based on the snapshot that David saw in the moment, and it's not useful or transferable to other lessons. In other words, the teacher would have to teach that same lesson again to implement David's feedback, which could happen in a subsequent period of the same subject matter or the following school year when the unit unfolds for the next batch of students. It's just not practical for teacher growth and development.

Luckily for David and his staff, he has a coach. His coach is a master at training administrators; in fact, they call him Yoda because of his ability to create other "Jedis." When David explains the problem, Yoda describes a concept called Principles of Instruction. *Basically, he recommends that a group of teachers come together and analyze the most important learning and teaching structures, narrow them down to a set of principles, home in further for a focus, and then develop all of the teachers using specific models. Yoda reveals his experiences with this process whereby the teachers in schools with* Principles of Instruction *feel really good about their growth because all of the professional development and classroom visits are targeted in the same few areas. As they get better in those areas, they add new ones; it's much more of a mastery approach than the random feedback that they were getting prior to the development of the principles. David needs* Principles of Instruction *to ground his feedback and support his teacher, and Yoda is going to train him regarding how to do that.*

▶ YOU NEED A TARGET

David's style of feedback is more common than not. He's done a great job organizing his day through time-blocking so that he can get into classrooms frequently, which is working. Unfortunately for David, he falls into a perennial problem that school leaders create by not clearly communicating what they're looking for when they visit classrooms. Additionally, many school leaders don't have a clear set of instructional practices that they are looking for in classrooms for effective instruction. His teachers are frustrated by this, but not because they don't want feedback about how they can improve. They want clarity on what the school-based supervisors (principals and assistant principals) and instructional coaches are looking for. This typically happens because of three traps that school leaders are susceptible to.

▶ *Trap #1: Finding Your Look-Fors during the Visit*

Some school leaders—even those who know instructional practices well—don't have a clear plan when they visit teachers. They know that they need to be in classrooms, they know that their teachers need feedback, but too often miss this third ingredient, which is identifying and communicating the specifics of their focus before they enter the classroom. They're observing based on *what they see*, not *what they want to see*. That can create disastrous scenarios for both the observer and the teacher.

For the observer, it means that you have to process everything in real time as it's happening. That's already hard enough when you know what you're hoping to see; it's practically impossible if you don't have a preconceived notion about what should be unfolding behind the door as you enter. This is why the feedback ends up being mostly random. If you're just commenting on what you see without a shared expectation of the practices and engagement strategies that teachers should be using, your suggestions are mostly haphazard.

This makes it hard on the teacher because they don't know what to expect. It also makes it difficult to see and feel growth over time. If every visit is based on different and arbitrary feedback, progress is hard to make. Picking a target on the other hand allows the teacher to receive feedback in specific areas of focus so that incremental adjustments can be made to particular strategies that a teacher, or the whole school for that matter, is working on.

▶ Trap #2: Keeping Your Look-Fors a Secret

Sometimes school leaders know exactly what they want to see in classrooms. Maybe they're focused on a more student-centered approach, maybe they want to see more student collaboration, maybe they want to see direct instruction unfold a certain way. There are all kinds of instructional design approaches, many of which are backed by evidence and research. What we find, though, is that leaders haven't clearly communicated the instructional vision and what that looks like in the classroom. This can happen for a number of reasons.

There are times that the school leader isn't confident articulating their vision for classroom instruction; other times, it literally doesn't dawn on them to explain what they're looking for to the teachers. In the first case, it shouldn't fall entirely on the principal's shoulders to define the look-fors. In the second case, school leaders need the capacity to understand that the foundation of vision work is communication. Without a clear messaging to the staff and professional development on the instructional strategies that you want to see in classrooms, it's very typical for each teacher to approach instruction by using their own individual professional judgment, diffusing efforts, and creating vastly different student experiences from classroom to classroom. The better strategy is to reveal your instructional philosophy, create sound professional learning on the strategies, and identify clear classroom expectations on what the teaching and learning environment should look like, particularly what the teachers should be doing and what the students should be doing.

▶ *Trap #3: Relying on Your Memory*

We see all kinds of strategies when it comes to instructional leaders providing informal and formal feedback to teachers. The variance in formal observation structures from state to state and district to district is enormous. The informal structures can be even more dissimilar and often vary from school to school in the same district. For example, one school leader might write a quick message on a sticky-note while another school leader might have a special card that they fill out when visiting classrooms. We have even seen larger schools where two assistant principals in the same school provide their informal feedback using different methods to the same teachers.

The problem isn't necessarily the method for delivering the feedback but rather the lack of an inventory of what you've seen and what you're looking for from visit to visit. Without a catalog of your previous visits, you're relying on your memory to determine what you should say to the teacher. This means that you're not building on previous visits to help the teacher make incremental adjustments and you're having to remember the exact focus for that teacher or department. Relying on your working memory to recall the instructional focus, even if it's only one or two strategies for the whole year, is a tall order as you go from classroom to classroom. Doing so in accordance with each teacher's growth and development plan is utterly futile.

▶ CREATING AN INSTRUCTIONAL FOCUS

There are two remedies that can disentangle us from the traps above. The first is simple—school leaders need a way to catalog informal feedback to teachers so that they can review it for themselves and with the teachers so that their feedback and the teachers' practices are aligned with the instructional focus, and the teacher's skill level is improving. A cycle of continuous improvement requires feedback to be layered. Saying the same thing over-and-over or saying something new and different each time is never going to produce the incremental changes that lead to massive results. The easiest solution is email because it will allow you to sort by the teachers' names and the chronological order in which they received your previous feedback. That said, there are tons of web-based tools on the market for purchase that all have their pros and cons.

The second remedy is to establish a set of instructional priorities (we call them "Principles of Instruction") that all teachers are trained to use and that act as the foundation for how a lesson plan should unfold. Doing so is much more complex than switching to email as your documentation strategy for informal feedback, but the benefits are profound. This book is written in stepwise fashion. We address the instructional leader's time as the first step. Unlike Mara, David has the structures to get into classrooms. Mara's first step is to make classroom visits her priority, but David reveals that being out and about is not enough to successfully drive instruction in a positive way. What David needs is a sound set of *Principles of Instruction* to direct and guide the learning community. Without the ability to get into the most important spaces in our schools, it's not possible to lead instruction. That said, the establishment of a set of Principles of Instruction is necessary so that it can become the backbone of the visits and the feedback.

We want to acknowledge that while your best teachers will always make strides regardless of support, we contend that *all* teachers deserve and need regular feedback with predetermined goals for their growth. In fact, your superstars crave performance coaching more than the others. By having the instructional focus and a specific tool (Principles of Instruction), this enables teachers to become more reflective practitioners. Feedback from an object observer, based on clearly determined and consistent goals, is the best method we have in school to improve teacher practices, period. Using video and audio recordings are also good, and peer feedback can be powerful as well. But, when an instructional leader makes repeated visits to the same teachers' classrooms with a focus on particular pedagogical approaches to teaching and learning, and their feedback is layered and meaningful, nothing is more effective in improving student outcomes.

▶ THE TOOL: PRINCIPLES OF INSTRUCTION

Principles of Instruction are a set of standard teaching practices that we expect to see in lesson plans and pervasively used during walkthroughs and observations. There are a number of great books about what works in the classroom to engage students and to support the retention and transfer of information. That's not the aim of this book. In fact, we're not going to tell you, aside from a few examples, which strategies should be on your list of Principles of Instruction. You can lean on *Visible Learning* (2023) by John Hattie and his research, which can be found online. Hattie explains that almost all of the strategies that classroom teachers choose to use will work. The problem is that the average effect size is between 0.2 and 0.4, and there are many strategies that are above 0.4. We need teachers to select the strategies that work the best, and that's why we develop a set of Principles of Instruction as a guide for lesson planning.

We also point to *Powerful Teaching* by Bain and Agarwal. In this teacher-friendly book, the authors describe the science of learning, and they explain how the use of certain teaching strategies improves student cognition and memory. Again, there are free online resources available as well. The point is that instructional leaders must study what works and whittle down their expectations for classroom instruction into a clearly defined set of instructional practices that are designated as look-fors.

▶ *Setting a Vision*

The first step in creating your Principles of Instruction is to declare a vision for the classroom environment. For example, you may be a constructivist at heart, believing the theory that students learn by constructing their own knowledge versus passively taking in information. If that's the case, and the school community embraces it, then your Principles of Instruction vision statement will reflect a constructivist approach. Your statement might sound something like this: *We believe that students learn by doing and that project-based student-centered learning should be at the core of every lesson.*

Suppose you subscribe to the need for students to obtain 21st-century skills, such as critical thinking, creativity, collaboration, and communication. Your Principles of Instruction vision statement might be as follows: *We believe that every student should graduate with the durable skills necessary to be successful in life and work, including the ability to think critically, build creatively, collaborate with others, and communicate their ideas.*

The key to an instructional leadership vision statement is that it's attainable through the actions and plans of the teacher and the pedagogical strategies associated with teaching skills and imparting knowledge using specific Principles of Instruction. The last note regarding the creation of a Principles of Instruction vision statement is that it should be broad enough for any classroom in the school to implement, regardless of the content area, and once it's established, each department should build on the statement with their own vision for mathematics, science, CTE, etc., so it is relevant and available to them.

▶ Choosing the Principles

Once your vision statement is solidified, it's time to identify your school's *Principles of Instruction*. These are 8–10 principles and practices that you would like to see executed in every classroom, every day. You'll need to zoom out so that they're applicable to every discipline and zoom in so that they can be used to develop lesson plans. These should be observable practices in terms of what teachers and students are doing and saying during a classroom visit. They should be research and/or evidence based.

To select your principles, we suggest putting together a small team of people (6–8) who can represent the rest of the staff and disseminate after the *Principles of Instruction* are developed. If you don't already have an instructional leadership team, we encourage you to develop one. Effective teams can lead transformational change in a school. These folks should have access to the aforementioned tools—online resources, books, etc.—to "study" what works best and narrow down their list to about 8–10. One example of a principle is *feedback*. Whether it's peer-to-peer feedback, an online tool, or from the teacher, feedback is an essential aspect of learning. And, we would want to see feedback in every classroom every day. Another example is *chunking*. When information is scaffolded and broken down into smaller parts, it's easier to digest and more likely to be remembered.

A critical component in the design of *Principles of Instruction* is that the practices are named, defined, and described using clear examples. This means that communication methods are essential. Using slides, flipbooks, and even a website helps to bring the principles to life with clarity and meaning. The whole point is that the principles are the backbone to a great lesson plan without having to require a lesson plan format or even asking teachers to submit lesson plans. Because the principles should be visible in action during classroom visits, it should be simple to spot if teachers are planning lessons through the use of their *Principles of Instruction* materials (slides, flipbook, website, etc.).

▶ Selecting a Focus

It would be nice if everyone was an expert in the *Principles of Instruction* on day-one of their adoption, but that's not realistic. It's also not a reality that all the teachers will become experts in all of the principles in the first year that you use them. That's why we select an annual focus. Pick 2 or 3 of the principles and build your professional learning plans for the year around them. Let's look at a singular example of one principle as a focus.

Remember the sample vision statement from a previous section: *We believe that every student should graduate with the durable skills necessary to be successful in life and work, including the ability to think critically, build creatively, collaborate with others, and communicate their ideas.* Collaboration and communication are both written into the statement. It would make sense, then, to have *student discourse* as one of the principles. The next step is to provide your teachers with strategies and examples for how to effectively get students talking and sharing their ideas.

One really important example of a strategy that supports student discourse is the jigsaw method. It has a super high effect size on learning and retention, and, when done well, requires students to talk to one another in a structured way about course content. With student discourse as one of our focuses for the year, and the jigsaw as a strategy to ensure that it unfolds in both planning and classroom instruction, we need to build a model for how to do a jigsaw.

▶ Providing a Model

The model is what guides the users regarding the new focus. This is where things become granular, and it cannot be overlooked. Think back to David, he doesn't have look-fors, but even if he did create a vision, develop the Principles of Instruction with his team, select a clear focus, and identify a strategy, there's still no guarantee that the teachers would know how to use the strategy in practice. Again, this only leads to frustration for both the administrators and staff when the team identifies a strategy as a focus, and the teachers aren't using it. In cases like this, we tell administrators to lead with curiosity and determine why the strategy isn't being implemented prior to making unnecessary judgments or assumptions about the teachers.

Everything we discussed so far is the *what*; the model is the *how*. Let's look at two examples, the first being the jigsaw. Teachers need written and verbal directions. The best person for the job is an instructional coach, but not all schools have them. One of your teacher leaders can take charge. They'll need to put together materials first. We suggest laminated 3X5 cards on a ring whereby each card is a step in the process. On one side, the card signifies the step number, on the other, we provide directions. See below.

▶ *Jigsaw*

Step #1: The teacher introduces the topic and subtopics of the lesson. This can be done through direct instruction.

Step #2: Students are broken into "home groups," and each member of the home group is given a subtopic under the primary topic of the lesson.

Step #3: Students move to their "expert groups" to read about, study, and discuss their subtopics.

Step #4: After students have a grasp of their expert subtopics, they return to the home group to report their findings.

There are other nuances involved, like how students move and what materials they use, but the four main steps are clear, and everyone can use them to understand how the jigsaw works in practice.

▶ *Think-Pair-Share*

Another common collaborative structure is the think-pair-share. The problem is that teachers forget the think-time or lack direction on the pairing step. An incomplete think-pair-share strategy, such as not being intentional with the think-time, overlooks the power of metacognition and weakens the effectiveness of the strategy. But, if we develop a model, and the teachers follow it, everyone can be successful.

> Step #1: Think-Time—give students a designated number of seconds or minutes to think about the topic. Be sure to put a timer on the board and require silence.
> Step #2: Pair Up—use a process for pairing students, either predetermined pairs, numbered heads, shoulder partners, or some other distinct way to ensure that everyone has a partner and no one is wondering who their pair will be.
> Step #3: Sharing—after all students are partnered, make sure they know who shares first and for how long. Again, use a timer. If partner A goes first, they get a specific time to share their thoughts while partner B listens and then they switch on your command.

There are obviously other fun nuances to this, but the model guarantees that every teacher takes all of the appropriate steps to execute the strategy effectively and with fidelity. That said, it's still not enough for real teacher development to simply set them loose with the model and expect excellence. This may sound like a lot so far, but they still need more support than that.

▶ **Developing the Teacher**

Teachers need support to develop their practice to a standard of excellence in the classroom. The most important and fundamentally effective way to develop a teacher's practice is to observe and provide feedback. Fortunately, the feedback provider doesn't need to be as strong as the teacher being observed. The observation itself works to provide the "data" necessary to improve practice. The gold standard for observation is when two people—the observer and the teacher—can watch a recorded lesson together. The second-best option is for the observer to provide verbal feedback with a discussion, and the third-best option is when the observer can provide written feedback for the teacher.

Because of the logistics of the school day, the third option is the most feasible. In subsequent chapters, you'll learn how to provide meaningful feedback to improve teaching practices in a way that most school leaders are still inept at. Why? The reason is because most school leaders aren't trained in providing feedback. They're trained in the use of feedback tools—filling out paperwork and checking boxes, but not the language necessary to impact a change in behavior.

That said, the moment you train your teachers in the use of a new model, like the jigsaw or think-pair-share from the previous section, you're off to the races. You want to observe teachers as soon after they learn a new strategy as possible. This transforms the culture of the school from "I Gotcha" to "I Got You," because if they don't use the new methods that they learned within a week or two after learning them, they're not likely to use them, *ever*. And, if they don't get feedback in a timely fashion—praise and coaching—they'll only use the new strategies to a standard that they set, not necessarily the standards aligned with the vision for excellence. That's not because they have low standards or don't care, without feedback, they're doing their best and don't know any better. This is why it's imperative to train teachers on the use of the model and then provide feedback as the teachers practice the model in action as quickly as possible thereafter. It's the only way to develop teachers and sustain improvements.

> **LEADER WELL-BEING SIDE NOTE: COLLABORATION—THE KEY TO GREATER ACHIEVEMENT**
>
> Setting the Principles of Instruction vision is the only step in the 5-step process (setting a vision, choosing the principles, selecting a focus, providing a model, and developing the teacher) above that you might do on your own, and it can be created through a collaborative process as well, depending on your style. Everything else should be done with the assistance of teacher leaders and the administrative team. Don't burn yourself out by trying to accomplish everything all at once or by doing it all yourself.

▶ CONCLUSION

Principles of Instruction are the backbone of the look-fors you need when you visit classrooms. You cannot enact a vague or ambiguous vision, and your teachers certainly can't develop and execute lessons using strategies that they don't understand or can't implement. Too many leaders, like David, have a desire to be instructional leaders, but don't have the tools in place to reinforce their ideals. When David sets a clear vision, develops the principles to back it up, selects a focus area, and builds models for teachers to use, his eager teachers will happily demonstrate their new skills. That doesn't mean that he won't have a reluctant and skeptical bunch. We'll address that later in the book.

It does mean that the expectations are clear and the supports for changing practice are in place in a way that's transparent. Not only is it solid *instructional leadership*, having the vision and setting crystal clear expectations are just good *leadership* practices, in general. David isn't just improving his instructional leadership, he's becoming a better leader altogether.

▶ Next Steps Checklist

- Bring a team of trusted teacher leaders together and provide them with resources and materials to develop an instructional vision for every classroom in the school. A bonus step is to have each department or grade level use the new vision statement to create one for their subject or grade.
- The team can then use the vision to develop a set of principles that can be used for planning lessons to align what teachers and students are doing to the vision. Be sure that the principles are broad enough to apply to every classroom every day.
- Have the group select a focus principle (up to 3) for the school year. These 1–3 focal points will guide the professional development plans as well.
- Research and designate a pedagogical strategy or two that fall under each of the focus principles. When used

effectively, the strategies will support the principles in action to bring the vision to life for classroom instruction.
- Empower an instructional coach or a master teacher to build models for what the focus should look like and feel like as it unfolds for teachers and students. Each step should be clear and explicit.
- Be sure to observe teachers using the new models as soon as possible after they learn them. Every professional development opportunity should trigger a race for instructional leaders—principals, assistant principals, instructional coaches, specialists, etc.—to observe what the teachers learned in action in the classroom within days and weeks thereafter. Without observation and using a longer timeline will only render your professional development efforts a waste.

Reference

Hattie, J. (2023). *Visible learning: The sequel: A synthesis of over 2,100 meta-analyses relating to achievement.* New York: Routledge.

Part 2

Effective and Meaningful Feedback

4

Celebrating Teachers

▶ SANDY'S TEACHERS ARE DEFLATED

Sandy values and respects her teachers immensely, and she expects excellent student outcomes, which is why she pushes them to be at their best all the time. The problem is that her teachers don't feel like they can do anything right, and she is at a loss on how to fix it. They feel the pressure, but not the support. Unlike Mara, Sandy does a great job of getting into classrooms systemically, and unlike David, the school has documented Principles of Instruction, *and the communication around expectations couldn't be clearer. Even though Sandy's teachers are meeting expectations, many feel disconnected from her leadership. They feel like they're running hard but going nowhere, trapped in the motion of doing without the satisfaction of knowing if they're doing well. It's the classic hamster-on-a-wheel syndrome: effort without fulfillment.*

Sandy is a visionary when it comes to instructional leadership. When she took over the school, the first thing that she did was to bring teachers together to develop their Principles of Instruction. *She knew that teachers and students cannot hit a moving target. As such, they started with a school-wide vision for what every classroom should look like, and then each department made their own vision statement aligned to it. Her team developed a set of strong* Principles of Instruction, *and they've had a focus area every year since she's been the principal. Her instructional coach creates models for each of the focal points, does professional development aligned to the models, and the school leaders are reinforcing the models by doing walkthroughs for every teacher once a week with feedback each time.*

The problem is that the teachers only feel the weight of the pressure and not any of the support by way of encouragement, reassurance, validation. Every visit seems to come with more recommendations and not the relief in knowing that their efforts are paying off or even appreciated. Whenever Sandy hears this sentiment from her leadership team, she's perplexed. She always tells them how much she cares about them, and she's quick to tell them that they're doing a great job. She even has an Outstanding Effort Award *that she gives out once a month at faculty meetings.*

The teachers, on the other hand, have no idea if the risks that they're taking with the new strategies or the execution of them are valued or even recognized. Sandy's goal-oriented mindset, while well-intentioned, leads her into the familiar trap of tunnel vision—where outcomes take priority over people. Her issue is twofold: Sandy's praise within her instructional feedback lacks specificity, and too often, it's an afterthought. Her praise is too general. Offering vague compliments like "great job" or "keep up the great work" fall short of the descriptive praise that people need and want as feedback. She needs a model of her own so that she can get better at providing feedback to the teachers just like they're using a model to improve their classroom instruction.

Fortunately for Sandy, and her staff, she has the same coach as David and Mara. One of Yoda's jobs is to review Sandy's feedback and provide feedback to her about it. Yoda notices that Sandy doesn't use praise well. She uses it, but she's not specific, and she seems to be focused on compliance rather than empowerment. Yoda shows her a model that changes everything.

▶ YOUR FEEDBACK ISN'T LANDING

Sandy's feedback in the form of praise isn't functioning the way in which she intends. Her teachers know that she sets a very high bar for classroom instruction, but they never know when they reach it. Her newest teachers, her best teachers, and everyone in between are only feeling the pressure that Sandy communicates and not her appreciation for their hard work. It's not that Sandy doesn't want to celebrate her people; she's very sensitive to their needs and building a culture where people want to work. It's that she falls into three very common traps that we find in schools where the principal is doing everything possible to be an instructional leader.

▶ *Trap #1: Lacking Specificity*

The biggest stumbling block when praise isn't being received the way it's intended is that it lacks specificity. Effective praise reinforces and celebrates a specific action, and without specificity, the person being praised is left uncertain to what is praiseworthy. Saying "great job" or "excellent work" is too vague and ambiguous for the receiver to understand how their performance will lead to greater student achievement. At best, it offers a sense of relief by acknowledging that the teacher's performance wasn't bad but does nothing to reinforce professional growth.

The fundamental problem with vague praise and recognition is it's not actionable. Feedback that is anchored to expected outcomes instructs and guides the teacher. If a sales associate lands a big deal, and the manager praises her for the effort and persistence with the client, noting the importance of the deal for the firm's stability, that's clear enough for the associate to repeat their effort and persistence in the future. Persistence is recognized as the key driver of success. Too often teachers aren't provided with examples of the key drivers that are yielding great results in their classroom.

At worst, a lack of specificity with praise can complicate the administrator-teacher relationship. Because the art and science of teaching is nuanced, vague praise can even be condescending.

We once heard from a teacher who received a $25 gift card from her principal with a note that said, "keep up the great work," and she literally burned the card since she felt that the administrator was out of touch and that the gift was an empty attempt to connect.

We fully realize that this is an extreme account, but it's also a true story of real frustration. The point is that teaching is a highly skilled profession with so many details required for lesson planning, relationship building, classroom management, content knowledge, technical prowess, and more. Hence, without specific praise, teachers don't receive the high-level guidance and coaching required to excel in the classroom and repeat the actions that yield student success and discontinue those that don't.

▶ Trap #2: Praising the Wrong Outcomes

Another powerful reason to use specific praise is the psychological impact of reinforcing wanted behaviors and actions, which we'll come back to later in this chapter. This means that praising specific practices will lead to the receiver repeating those actions again in the future. Consequently, if we praise the wrong behaviors, we run the risk of promoting unwanted outcomes. This leads to the opposite of effective instructional leadership. We're no longer improving instruction, we're promoting the status quo or making it worse.

In general, it's important to praise teachers for two separate but equally important reasons: effort and excellence. The first is *effort*. We want teachers to take risks and try new instructional strategies or tools that could make a difference for the learner. Just as teachers create safe places for students to learn, administrators must create safe places for teachers to teach. Consider the jigsaw strategy, an effective learning strategy, but equally challenging for teachers to master. Imagine the jigsaw being taught to teachers during a professional learning session, and you see a teacher attempting to implement it that same week, even if it is executed poorly, it's a positive act and worthy of *effort praise*.

Here is an example of effort-based praise:

I really appreciate the way you jumped in and tried the jigsaw strategy with your class so soon after the professional development. It takes courage to try something new, and your willingness to experiment shows real commitment to professional growth and student engagement. Thank you.

The second form of praise is *excellence*. It's critical to remember, though, that we only get to excellence through effort, which is why these are inextricably connected with one another. If you observe one of your superstar teachers using the jigsaw activity with precision and accuracy, then an excellence feedback statement is required.

Here is an example of excellence-based praise:

Your use of the jigsaw strategy was outstanding. The way you structured the heterogeneous groups, paired with clear learning targets, and structured student collaboration created a real learning opportunity for student discourse. The materials you selected were engaging and accessible for all learners, and you clearly amplified student voice in the process. It's a textbook example of what effective, student-centered instruction looks like. Fantastic work.

The skill is to be able to delineate between the two types of praise with technical feedback that effectively reinforces the desired actions, attitudes, and outcomes (AAOs). When leaders mix these two up—praising for excellence when effort was used to try something new (and not done with precision) or praising for effort when the teacher was demonstrating instructional precision—the consequences are detrimental. The leader could inadvertently reinforce mediocrity, limiting teacher growth for the average teacher, or fail to provide excellence praise to the highly effective teacher, leaving them with a hollow feeling and missing an opportunity to drive school-wide excellence. We'll come back to this concept of effort and excellence later in the book.

▶ Trap #3: Using Praise Sparingly

Even when we teach people the power of praise, and even when they understand the model that you're about to learn, they still don't use it enough. Whether it's a fear regarding staff dynamics with some people getting too much praise or a worry that praise dilutes high standards, some leaders limit their praise. Regardless of the reason, it's scarcity thinking, and that's a trap. The truth is that you can't give enough praise to people as long as it's done for effort or excellence using the specific praise model that you'll learn in the coming pages. Meaningfully crafted praise is always a successful way to improve morale, maintain high standards, identify teacher strengths, reinforce goals, create coherence, and raise the instructional ability of every teacher.

Some leaders believe that praise will make their people complacent—the praise will result in folks doing less because they think they've "arrived." Again, this is a trap. In fact, authentic praise reinforces growth. One thing to be careful about with praise is that it will build a culture that expects to receive it. In other words, the more praise you use, the more people will work hard to get it, and the more they will be disappointed in themselves when you don't provide it. Praise doesn't lead to laziness; it leads to a stronger work ethic on the team.

Lastly, leaders are often afraid that too much praise, especially for the people who have so many improvements to make, will downplay the significant work that they have to do to become better. But, this is also a trap. Effort praise can and should be encouraging. The reality is that our novice teachers are often our most vulnerable. When a leader hesitates to offer praise, that same teacher may be silently struggling, feeling unseen, questioning their impact, and quietly exploring other jobs. A few words of specific encouragement could be the difference between losing a staff member and cultivating excellence. We are better off heeding the advice of Jim Marshall, author of *Right from the Start*, who says that any important initiative should start with the bright spots. It's critical to highlight what we're doing well early in the implementation so that we can collect early wins to motivate us to continue on the journey.

▶ UNLOCKING THE POWER OF SPECIFIC PRAISE

One of the most important things to learn about praise is the value that it has for the leader and the school as a whole. This is counterintuitive because we naturally think of praise as having value for the receiver, which is true, but it doesn't stop there. Leaders who don't use, misuse, or misunderstand praise are doing so because they don't understand why it's critical to organizational success. Simon Sinek (2009) teaches leaders that without a compelling rationale—a *why*—people don't budge from their old ways. This holds true for the leaders themselves.

When we teach leaders the professional and organizational benefits of using specific praise, they typically change their behavior to include it regularly in their feedback. Let's dive in. We already established that *effort* and *excellence* are the *what* when using specific praise, now let's get into the *why*. There are two main benefits of effective praise. The first is that it stimulates an emotional response in a feeling of a job well done. Pride is a positive emotion that occurs after a specific accomplishment, and leaders who use praise well instill pride in the people they're praising. In the workplace, pride improves psychological conditions that lead to self-esteem and social connection. This is important for the organization—in this case a school—because it results in a greater degree of satisfaction and motivation. The result is a greater degree of productivity.

The second reason for praise is to reinforce behaviors. That said, we have to do it right. Cognitive scientists, including Daniel Willingham in his book entitled *Why Don't Students Like School* (2021), have identified the limits of self-reflection. Although personal reflection is touted as key to growth, it's not as simple as we think. It's unlikely that teachers are reflecting on their work as it unfolds. It's hard to assess how you're doing, while you're actually doing the work. That is why people so often ask the simple question after any performance, "how'd I do?"

When we're busy working, our brains are focused on what we're doing, not on how well we're doing it. This translates to a lack of clarity around which strategies should be repeated—one reason why we see teachers not necessarily duplicating their best practices even when they are highly effective. It's very possible that they don't know what they're doing that is working well. This is why athletes study film. It leads to precise performance-based learning. A skilled observer, on the other hand, can identify and acknowledge something that went well, and specific praise will reinforce the behavior so that it's repeated in subsequent lessons. This is a benefit to the organization because it illuminates the teaching moves that should be used habitually, reinforces them, and helps them to permeate the whole staff.

Hence, specific praise is as much in service of the leader, the vision, and the organizational goals as it is the receiver. The rationale for using it moves beyond making people feel good, although that's a perfectly fine reason to do it. The point is that leaders who need convincing or who think that praising people is a "nice to have" rather than a "have to have," should think otherwise.

▶ THE TACTIC: SPECIFIC PRAISE MODEL

Making the decision to use Specific Praise more often is the first step. The second step is to understand that crafting praise statements that result in the benefits raised above—authentic pride and repeated behaviors—is a skill. While there are leaders who know about the importance of praise and still don't use it, there are other leaders who say that they use praise only to realize that their employees don't feel that they're being praised. In other words, leaders who are apt to use specific praise don't do it well enough for it to work. Precisely the problem with Sandy's feedback and the culture of pressure without the feeling of support that she's creating.

That's why we built our model for specific praise. Using the model, improves your ability to craft language—written or verbal—that instructs and guides the receiver in the way that you intend. If you're going to increase the amount of praise you give, it's also important to enhance the way that you do it. We built the model below based on research regarding neuroscience, behavioral psychology, and effective communication. We know two things for sure: one, the model works, and, two, it takes practice to get good at using it (Figure 4.1).

▶ *The Model*

The Specific Praise model has four parts, and we're going to explain all four parts and why each of them is important to the overall delivery of your sentiments.

▶ *Part 1: Make a Praise Statement*

The first part of the specific praise model is a "praise statement." We're leading with an assurance that the receiver understands that what we're about to say is meant to lift their spirits and support their work. Because humans are naturally inclined to find what's wrong with themselves and the world, we're always

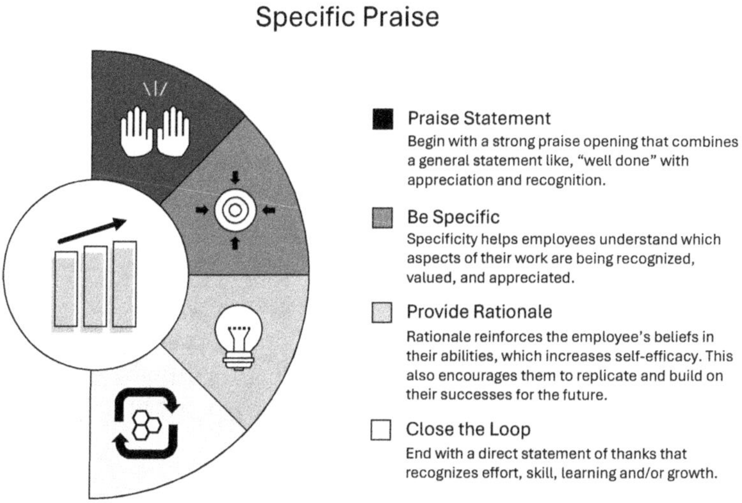

Specific Praise

■ Praise Statement
Begin with a strong praise opening that combines a general statement like, "well done" with appreciation and recognition.

■ Be Specific
Specificity helps employees understand which aspects of their work are being recognized, valued, and appreciated.

□ Provide Rationale
Rationale reinforces the employee's beliefs in their abilities, which increases self-efficacy. This also encourages them to replicate and build on their successes for the future.

□ Close the Loop
End with a direct statement of thanks that recognizes effort, skill, learning and/or growth.

Figure 4.1 Specific Praise

bracing ourselves for bad news. We open the specific praise model with a praise statement to avoid any confusion about the message that we're getting ready to deliver.

A praise statement can range from "Fantastic work today!" to "Thank you for an excellent job with this lesson." The problem with the praise statement alone, as discussed previously, is that by itself it can potentially do more harm than good. "Fantastic work" and "excellent job" are ambiguous, and ambiguity with praise can result in meaningless feedback and even resentment. It's meaningless because we don't know what was fantastic or excellent, and it can spark resentment when someone takes it to be a sign that we aren't aware of the nuanced contribution that they make each day. This is where Part 2 of the model comes into play.

▶ Part 2: Be Specific

The second part of the Specific Praise model is a detail regarding the specific action, attitude, or outcome (AAO) that was observed, and they generally fall into those three categories—AAOs. Actions are the behaviors that we observe people exhibiting. Attitude is the emotional state in which they work. Outcomes are the results of their effort.

The more granular the better because you want the receiver to be able to repeat that exact desired behavior in the future. If you're too general here, you risk that the person might interpret what you're saying only to replicate something a bit different than what you meant. If what you're praising is something so important for this person to continue doing, you have to describe it with precision.

The last aspect of Part 2 of the model, which you'll recall from the Traps, is to praise for either *effort* or *excellence*, and to never mistake one for the other. If, for example, the AAO involves a risk that the person is taking to try something new—possibly something they just learned from an instructional coach—but it's not a fully developed skill yet, you should praise their *effort*. If, on the other hand, the person is really executing at the highest standard, you should praise for *excellence*. We'll define this further when we get to the examples.

▶ Part 3: Provide a Rationale

The third part of the specific praise model is to provide a rationale for why the AAO is so critical to the success of the team. Ask yourself: why is this AAO of importance to our school? What is it about the *effort* that the person is demonstrating or the *excellence* with which they work that deems it worthy of praise?

The answer to these types of questions is the rationale that gets placed in the third section of your feedback message. It works to make the feedback more meaningful, but it also empowers the receiver because it's a reminder about the bigger picture. The rationale is the purpose behind the AAOs. Without the rationale, specificity alone will work to reinforce a behavior, but it will only do so at a level of compliance. The rationale equips the receiver with a greater degree of motivation, which is important so that they don't just comply in the future because you said so but because they want to.

▶ Part 4: Close the Loop

The final step in the model is to do what we call "closing the loop." The loop opens with a praise statement and then closes with one as well. There's a really important reason for this, which is to ensure that the receiver understands that you're celebrating their work. This specific praise model is sophisticated in nature and predicated on the science of the brain. What we know is that humans are looking for danger. We're wired to identify the things that will cause either physical or emotional harm and then prevent or avoid them from happening. This is often called our "lizard brain" or amygdala, which is a key structure of our limbic system that controls fear, flight, fight, and other responses to possible uncertainty and risk.

In the absence of a final praise statement, such as "I'm impressed with your work today, thank you!" the receiver has the potential to begin wondering what they did wrong or what you're trying to identify that needs improvement without actually saying it. The lizard brain does that naturally and is compounded by experiences with the feedback sandwich, which combines praise with something to improve, followed up with more praise. This strategy is rooted in leaders' desire to soften the blow of a negative comment, and it doesn't work as praise or performance coaching. In fact, it's about the worst thing you can do if you want feedback to make a difference for the future of someone's behavior at work. In the next section, we provide four examples of specific praise, and we'll unpack each regarding the AAOs that we're looking to reinforce.

▶ **Examples**

▶ **Example #1**

It was great being here for the jigsaw today. I truly appreciate that you implemented this strategy so quickly after our professional development that Olivia modeled at the last faculty meeting. It's so important that we take risks to improve our instructional abilities through the use of recently learned strategies, especially those with such high effect sizes on learning like this one. Thank you so much for making our PD efforts a priority for implementation in your classroom.

The first praise statement opens the loop: *It was great being here for the jigsaw today.* This sets the stage for the feedback in that it's effort praise and not something to improve upon. This approach calms the lizard brain by reducing worry or fear and establishes the appropriate context so the teacher can accept the praise. It's then very specific with the next statement: *I truly appreciate that you implemented this strategy so quickly after our professional development that Olivia modeled at the last faculty meeting.* This is praise for effort on the part of the teacher and not excellence. The rationale comes next as the third part of the model: *It's so important that we take risks to improve our instructional abilities through the use of recently learned strategies, especially those with such high effect sizes on learning like this one.* We're looking to empower the teacher to take risks, try new strategies, and implement highly effective practices. And, the loop is closed with a final praise statement: *Thank you so much for making our PD efforts a priority for implementation in your classroom.*

▶ Example #2

It was a privilege being in your class today and seeing the jigsaw activity in action. It was super impressive that the students understood the concept of their "home" versus "expert" groups so well and could explain them to me. It's important that they grasp the details of the strategy as the learners so that they take greater ownership of their learning, while developing transferable skills for future use. You executed today's lesson with excellence and precision; nice work.

In Example 1, we're praising for effort; in Example 2, we're praising for excellence. The opening statement in Example 2 denotes praise: *It was a privilege being in your class today and seeing the jigsaw activity in action.* We're doubling down on praise again in the second sentence and adding the specificity: *It was super impressive that the students understood the concept of their "home" versus "expert" groups so well and could explain them to me.* It's fine to use one of the four parts multiple times. It's just not okay to skip one or more of the parts. In the third part of the model, we include a rationale, clearly indicating the importance of the precision: *It's important that they grasp the details of the strategy as the learners so that they take greater ownership of their learning, while developing transferable skills for future use.* The loop is closed with two more points of praise ("excellence" and "nice work"): *You executed today's lesson with excellence and precision; nice work.*

▶ Example #3

Fantastic work today. Your use of the co-teaching models we learned this year were implemented with clear purpose and precision. I watched you switch models twice in the time I was here today. It's so important that we use multiple models and not just one-teach, one-assist to support the different learners in our classrooms. I literally wouldn't have been able to tell which teacher is the general education versus special education. Very well done.

For this example, you can note the deviation from the simple four-part model to include more specificity and more rationale. The opening and closing of the loop should now be obvious. We're highlighting the use of the co-teaching models, but it's important to identify the reinforcement of professional development that the teachers experienced earlier in the school year. We'll revisit this strategy in Chapter 7. It should also be clear that in the past the teachers relied heavily on teach-and-assist, which has changed. This indicates a change in practice and the evolution of a continuous improvement model.

▶ *Example #4*

Wonderful work with the think-pair-share (TPS) today. I especially liked seeing the "think" part done so well. A lot of times, I see a TPS being used, and the think-time gets skipped or overlooked, which limits the metacognitive aspect of this strategy. You provided silent think-time and set a timer on the Smartboard for exactly how long you expected students to think before they paired and shared. It's incredibly important that students get that individual time and space to think in our classrooms. Love it!

For this example, you can identify the parts of the model on your own. What we want to highlight is what the observer uncovers as what she often sees versus what she prefers to see and the precision with a strategy like TPS. Not only does this reveal the observer's keen eye for the specifics of the strategy, it also elevates the teacher's practice above what's typical, communicating that this teacher is executing to a greater extent than her peers. We do this for two reasons: (1) We want our superstars to know that they're performing at a high level, which they're generally unaware of. (2) We want our top performers to know exactly what makes their instruction highly effective, and, in this case, it's the details in planning and developing instructional strategies.

> **LEADER WELL-BEING SIDE NOTE: TIMELINESS—HIT SEND BEFORE YOU LEAVE THE ROOM**
>
> As you conduct your classroom visits in accordance with your plan and you write feedback during those visits, be sure to be timely. Hit send on the email before you leave the room, log your feedback in the electronic form for teachers to access, or leave a 3x5 card note on the teacher's desk before departing. You want to do to yourself is procrastinate and risk getting backed up and never leaving feedback. And, the last thing you want your teachers to do is have their lizard brain kick in and distract them from the work they're doing because they are concerned with what you saw.
>
> First, that's not fair to the teachers as they eagerly await your words of affirmation, expectations for growth, and questions about their planning and what you observed. Second, it's not realistic that you will remember what you saw and be able to craft feedback after the fact.
>
> Not sending timely feedback diminishes the value for the teacher and creates after work stress for you. We refer to this as "hitting send before you leave the room," using whatever system you have to deliver the feedback. Hit send!

▶ CONCLUSION

When Sandy begins to practice the Specific Praise model, using all four parts each time, her teachers feel appreciated and celebrated. She moves past her general feedback and becomes much more granular in what she identifies in the effort and excellence of her staff. Her expectations are still very high, but the teachers now also feel appreciated. This balance of pressure and support, expectations and clarity, makes all the difference for instructional effectiveness, increased morale, and teacher retention. The model also makes Sandy a stronger instructional leader because it demands precision and discreet language that homes in on the particulars of the teacher's instruction.

What does this all mean for Sandy? She's seeing the fruits of her labor with the newfound pride that her teachers feel and the way that they're repeating, and even improving upon, the things she praises. She almost can't believe that the teachers are working to improve the aspects of their craft that she's praising. They're literally taking the bright spots and making them brighter. It's much easier to get better at the things we're already good at than to make improvements in areas of weakness, which is what we'll overcome with the next model in Chapter 5.

▶ Next Steps Checklist

- Conduct classroom visits with specific praise in mind. Look for bright spots to praise during every visit. What are your teachers doing well that they should be proud of and that you want to reinforce?
- When you're in a classroom and you identify a bright spot—attitudes, actions, or outcomes (AAOs)—decide whether it's *effort* on the part of the teacher or *excellence* in terms of execution. Don't confuse the two.
- Use your four-part model—praise statement, specificity, rationale, praise statement—to write praise in an email or other method.
- Be sure to check your four-part model to ensure you used all four parts at least once each and in the write order.
- Send the message, leave the note, or log the praise in your system. Hold yourself accountable to providing the praise for the teacher before you leave the room.

References

Marshall, J. (2023). *Right from the start: The essential guide to implementing school initiatives.* Thousand Oaks, CA: Corwin.

Sinek, S. (2009). *Start with why: How great leaders inspire everyone to take action.* New York: Penguin Random House.

Willingham, D. (2021). *Why don't students like school? A cognitive scientist answers questions about how the mind works and what it means for the classroom.* San Francisco, CA: Jossey-Bass.

Making Incremental Progress

▶ LARA'S TEACHERS NEED A COACH

Lara fully realizes the power of specific praise and how her feedback is not just about making teachers feel good. She knows that praise boosts morale, helps teachers repeat effective strategies, and develops a culture of continuous improvement. She's been at West Side Elementary for three years and her teachers love her. She possesses some amazing qualities as a leader that her staff respond to well. She's direct and caring, with high expectations balanced with support. She's in classrooms often and provides feedback. Her praise is heartfelt and specific, she recognizes a smooth transition from the desks to the carpet, acknowledges an engaging warm-up activity, or a smooth interaction with a reluctant student. Unfortunately, there's still a problem.

Lara's critical performance feedback is not moving the needle. Her praise is spot on, but her expectations for change are blurry, often creating confusion over clarity. What's difficult for Lara is that the teachers aren't changing because they're reluctant, they want to grow. The lack of change is mostly because they are struggling to interpret what Lara wants them to do differently.

This was a huge revelation after a round of walkthroughs in the fall. The focus was on increasing student discourse through structured conversations about the content of the lesson. Lara wasn't seeing the level of questioning needed to have the students use reasoning or defend an idea with a peer. The questions were still predominantly at the recall level and not creating opportunities for students to really engage at a high level.

After her walkthroughs, she sent teachers an email, clearly identifying what she saw, but during her second round of visits, she wasn't seeing any change. It finally hit her when her assistant principal gently shared, "the staff loves hearing from you, but they're trying to guess what you mean." When the mid-year assessment data report was released and student scores were flat, she knew that it was more than just the teachers who needed to make a change. She had her own work to do to improve her feedback.

Lara was in luck. The district was using a master coach, Yoda, that she was able to spend some time with. In the first session, Lara admitted that her constructive feedback wasn't working and that she needed help. Yoda dove right in by asking poignant questions on how she provided feedback—email, post-it note, verbally, etc. Lara revealed that she mostly just sent an email. As they reviewed some of the feedback, Yoda quickly realized the difference between her praise and constructive feedback. Her praise was specific and precise, while her suggestions for improvement were broad, vague, and generally too soft.

Yoda smiled and let her know that they were going to turn her into an architect—equipping her with the ability to create blueprints for change. It would be something that her staff could easily follow and be clear on the expectations. Yoda quickly took one example and outlined how her feedback suggested that a teacher "increase student engagement" but did not provide clarity regarding an actual strategy, such as "have students answer three open-ended questions in a small group rotation." It became apparent that Lara knew in her mind what she wanted the teachers to change but her communication and explanations were ambiguous.

Lara saw the difference and chuckled, knowing she would learn a lot from Yoda in the coming weeks. Better yet, Yoda unpacked a powerful four-step process for effective Performance Coaching designed to ignite real change in practice. Lara was excited and a little nervous, but deep down she knew that this was exactly what she needed to make the progress she envisioned.

▶ YOU'RE COACHING METHODS AREN'T MAKING CHANGE

Lara's not alone in her inability to provide her teachers with very intentional Performance Coaching feedback. It requires a high level of skill, not only from an instructional vantage point, but from a communication perspective that strips away guesswork and eliminates vagueness. Knowing *what to change* is vastly different from knowing *how to change* it. Communicating that change is a real challenge for many school leaders. The devil really is in the details, and effective coaching requires a clear tool for feedback that changes teachers' practice. Too often administrators provide unclear, fuzzy feedback, with little direction. Or, they'll dance around an issue hoping that the instruction will improve through some other means. We find that leaders fall into three traps when failing to provide effective Performance Coaching.

▶ *Trap #1: Avoiding the Conflict*

One of the most prevalent traps that leaders fall into is conflict avoidance. The reality is that many leaders clearly see what the issue is, yet, they often sidestep the problem. Whether it's fear that the conflict will escalate, become overly dramatic, or damage a relationship, the deficiencies aren't dealt with, persist, and even get worse.

Most educators enter the profession to serve, to help, to guide others, while building strong and positive relationships. Directly confronting a person can feel completely unnatural and run counter to their beliefs. Conflict, even when healthy and productive, can feel unnatural. If a leader's identity is tied to being supportive, then avoiding a direct conflict will feel like the right approach.

This internal conflict, essentially a moral tug-of-war, rests on the notion that by directly addressing a person and a problem, the relationship can be permanently damaged, the problem won't be solved and might negatively impact teacher morale. This fear forces the leader to question herself and her ability to incrementally make progress, which creates doubt and hesitation. Worse yet, if the leader has tried confronting someone in the past and it went south, the leader now has "evidence" that this approach doesn't work. This is untrue and likely due to the leader's coaching skills and not the inevitable negative outcome in conflict.

Unfortunately, this trap protects ineffective practices, erodes growth, and sends signals to the staff that poor performance is acceptable. Progress is stifled and mediocrity ensues. The challenge is to reframe the conflict so that it is not viewed as "hurting" a person but rather as helping them and their students.

▶ Trap #2: Easing into the Conversation

Another prominent trap is building walls of confusion and misdirection to avoid tackling the problem head on. Many leaders will muster up the courage to confront an issue, but when it comes time to have the conversation, they ease into it by using small talk and niceties for so long that the issue is never presented. This is another avoidance behavior. What makes this one particularly challenging is that the leader can convince themselves that this is how we demonstrate respect and care before confronting a problem—by easing in and "lessening the blow," attempting to have a tough conversation, but then reverting back to "protecting" the relationship.

Sadly, this doesn't work. When the conversation is couched with so much other information, the real intent and purpose of the conversation is lost. Even worse, the leader may even confuse the person and leave them thinking that everything is fine. These conversations typically start with a preamble of sorts, maybe the weather, maybe sports, maybe something else that's going on in the school. They may even start with a compliment. After some lengthy banter, the leader brings up the issue and then minimizes it in some fashion by offering reassurances.

This lack of candor dilutes the message, creates ambiguity, and leaves no next steps for improvement or progress. The harsh reality with this approach is that the leader is actually protecting themselves. They don't want to be uncomfortable, they don't want to be the "bad guy" and unfortunately without clarity nothing changes. The other debilitating hidden cost is that the leader loses respect from the person and the staff. Tough conversations require courage and precision, candor and compassion, empathy and support. Small talk has a place, but it's certainly not within a Performance Coaching scenario. It's in the concession stand while helping to sell hot dogs or during the after-school soccer game, not when addressing a critical need to change practice.

▶ Trap #3: Staying Too General

The third trap is just as prevalent if not more so than the other two, with many leaders falling victim to being too general in their feedback and coaching. This happens when the leader is so vague that the person receiving the information has no clue about what the issue really is or what needs to change. The feedback typically sounds like: "you should work on getting more students involved." Or "Are your lessons challenging enough?" Or "You should tighten up your classroom management."

To the leader, these statements and questions may seem clear, but they are not supported with an accurate account of what occurred or the necessary details of the situation. There is no precision or clarity. Great feedback creates a road map for the receiving person so next steps aren't a mystery. General statements like the ones above also assume the teacher knows what meaningful engagement looks like, how to measure the rigor of an assignment, or create structures and systems to improve classroom management. Those assumptions maintain the status quo by failing to provide actionable steps for the teacher to take in the future.

After the feedback is sent or the conversation occurs, the leader may even assume that the teacher fully understands the issue and how to fix it. The better assumption to make is that if the teacher knew what the problem was and how to fix it herself, she would have already done so. Some leaders suffer from being too general because they view detailed next steps as "micromanaging." They may even disguise their lack of clarity as providing teachers with autonomy. Unfortunately, all this does is to prevent the school from making incremental progress over time that leads to overall school improvement and better student outcomes.

▶ DRIVING PROGRESS THROUGH PERFORMANCE COACHING

Effective Performance Coaching for school leaders is centered on improving teachers' skills in a particular area of their instructional practice. It's challenging to master because it's not simply telling someone what to do, rather, it's actually helping them see what to improve and then guiding and teaching them *how* to improve it. Effective feedback enables and empowers teachers by identifying blind spots, revealing a new or different approach, and helping them to be at their best for their students, something all teachers want for themselves and their kids. The power of the observation is that the instructional leader can see something that needs improvement that the teacher might never identify without the support of the observer.

The only way to create this meaningful change in practice is for the leader to make the necessary time to visit classrooms, identify a need for change, and provide meaningful feedback to teachers on what, why, and how to make the change. In this section, we're going to reframe how you think about corrective feedback as an instructional leader so that you see this process as a key driver of excellence and the avenue to create lasting impact on teacher moves and student outcomes.

Corrective feedback lives as the intersection of candor and compassion. Feedback has to be clear enough to understand and take action but delivered in a way that dignity and professionalism remain intact. There are two aspects of this work that school leaders must come to embrace. The first thing that instructional leaders have to reframe in their mind is that without quality Performance Coaching, we stall progress, limit growth, and impede student achievement. We have to overcome the traps outlined above to lead learning in our school. We're not creating conflict, we're overcoming it.

Second, leaders have to accept that there is typically a wide gap between the constructive feedback that they provide and a teacher's ability to know what to do with the information. While leaders may think that their feedback is clear, it usually comes with what we call a *muddy point*. A *muddy point* in feedback occurs when the message makes sense conceptually, but the person isn't sure how to turn it into action. They understand the problem, but the next steps are unclear, leaving them without a concrete path forward.

Hence, the biggest problems with coaching stem from our ability to see ourselves as a true leader of learning, helping teachers to improve practice, and the clarity in how teachers should make a change to instruction. The following step-by-step coaching model is designed to help instructional leaders overcome both problems.

▶ THE TACTIC: PERFORMANCE COACHING MODEL

Performance Coaching begins with a mindset that everyone can and should improve. This mindset drives culture and, done effectively, builds a thriving, growth oriented environment. Leaders need to clearly establish that this is one of the primary ways that teachers grow. This is really no different than the mindset we want students to have—that learning requires a deliberate and structured approach so that their abilities and talents are nurtured and developed. Our Performance Coaching model is designed to anchor the area of improvement in an established standard or expectation, clearly stated and understood rationale for the change, and, most importantly, supported with how to make the change, resources, expectations, and accountability. It is essentially a pressure and support model that relies on expertise, trust, and faith in one another to improve practice (Figure 5.1).

▶ The Model

The Performance Coaching model has four parts, and we're going to explain all four parts and why each of them is important to the overall delivery of your feedback.

Performance Coaching

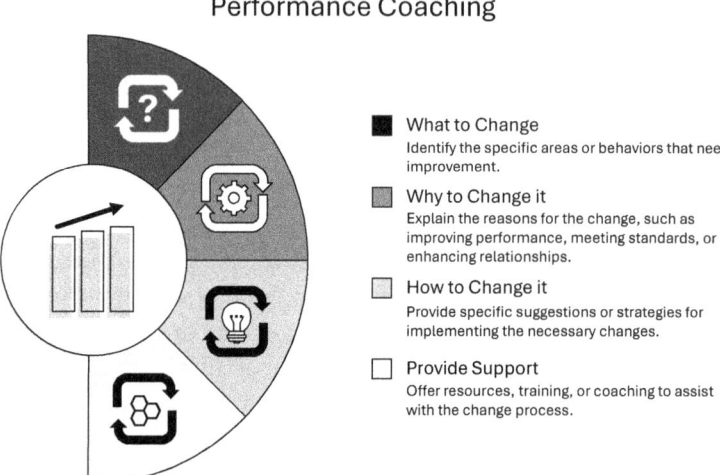

Figure 5.1 Performance Coaching

▶ *Part 1: What to Change*

The model begins with something that the teacher needs to change. This is an objective description of what you saw. There are three broad areas that change usually falls within: (1) The overall classroom culture; (2) Fidelity with the curriculum; and (3) The instructional strategies that are expected to be in use through either school or district Principles of Instruction (PoI) or recently delivered professional development that should be in place.

We cannot emphasize enough how vital it is to anchor corrective feedback in these areas. Well run schools and districts have these three aspects of instruction clearly outlined and developed so that there is no mystery regarding what is expected from the teachers' daily work. Framing feedback within these areas removes any personal preferences because the expectations are school-wide and predefined. It's not about what the administrator wants or prefers; it's about the shared standards that apply to everyone.

When supervisors or observers begin the model, they should pick the most high leverage change to improve the teacher's delivery. For example, if there was a missed opportunity for a collaborative structure, and that would have improved student engagement and understanding, that should be *what* we identify as the change that's needed. Again, the model begins with an objective "what to change," based on the observation.

▶ Part 2: Why to Change

The next step is to focus on *why* the change is necessary and how it benefits the students or the school. There are numerous studies and research available that affirms and identifies best practices. Administrators cannot assume that everyone knows or understands the research, which is why the explanatory, instructive component is critical. It enables the teacher to fully understand why the change to practice is important.

Consider a school with literacy as their focus for the year with a particular concentration on highly effective strategies such as the Socratic seminar. During an observation, months into the school year, a veteran health teacher is still using round-robin reading. The administrator must address this for two primary reasons: first, literacy is every teacher's responsibility; and second, the research is clear that round-robin reading remains at a surface-level, creates disengagement for many students, and is low-impact on comprehension. A Socratic seminar, on the other hand, requires deep analysis, collaboration, and engagement. As such, the observer would have identified the round-robin strategy as the *what to change* and then explain that there are more effective strategies, *why to change*, such as the Socratic seminar, which yields better results based on research. Establishing this *why to change* creates a healthy sense of pressure, but it's incomplete in terms of support unless we help the teacher with *how to change* and the associated *resources* with the change.

▶ Part 3: How to Change

The third step in the process is where the partnership and trust within this performance feedback coaching model thrives. Change is hard, especially for educators. Since many teachers hold much of their identity within their profession, even the most growth-minded, constructive criticism can be perceived as, "what I've been doing isn't good enough?" This reality, coupled with other real challenges—such as initiative fatigue, cognitive load, and the belief that there is a lack of autonomy—all create genuine obstacles that can thwart improvement.

As previously mentioned, we cannot assume that teachers know *how* to change even when they know *what* to change. While that's not always the case and there will be times when an administrator finds themselves in a situation where they are facing an obstinate employee who decides to dig their heels in, most teachers are open to altering their practice to support student learning, which requires demonstration, modeling, coaching, resources, tools, and time. We'll come back to defensive and resistant teachers in Chapter 8.

Let's come back to the case of the round-robin reading being replaced with a Socratic seminar. The teacher knows what needs to change and even what to do differently, but we cannot assume that they know how to implement a Socratic seminar. In this step of the feedback model, we will literally provide directions for using a Socratic seminar that we would believe the teacher could follow in a subsequent lesson to at least try the strategy for themselves.

▶ Part 4: Provide Support

The fourth step is arguably the most important. We would never take the training-wheels off a bike, sit our child on the seat, push them down the road, and then turn our back on them. Yet, if we offer critical feedback, expecting different actions and behaviors from our teachers, but don't offer support and guidance, then that is exactly what we are doing to them. We need to create a system of support that helps them along the way.

This system is grounded in suggestions about where they might go to get more information. We can suggest an article about the use of Socratic seminars and link it in the feedback. We can ask them to visit a peer who uses Socratic seminars often and with excellence. Or, we might simply invite them to further the conversation if they don't fully understand. Frequent check-ins, discussions on how suggestions have worked out, and ongoing encouragement is a must. This directly ties back to our Specific Praise model. We praise effort and excellence. When we support growth through Performance Coaching, we're asking teachers to make a new effort, one that we hope we can revisit for Specific Praise.

> ## LEADERSHIP WELL-BEING SIDE NOTE: CLEAR EXPECTATIONS—DON'T BE TIMID TO PROVIDE SUPPORT
>
> Take a moment and think about a doctor withholding vital health information because they are worried about how their patient would receive the news. The thought of it is unconscionable. We want you to embrace the same belief system—you're the leader and the expert in many ways. Granted, a teacher may have the content expertise, but great school leaders know how to elevate every teacher, most importantly their best. Consistently evoke your high standards—they're not off-putting, they're uplifting. Demand excellence. Your best teachers will thank you, others will surprise you, and some will realize that another opportunity may be in their (and their students) best interest.
>
> Free yourself from the worry that clear expectations might bruise a relationship and come to the realization that it can strengthen them. Leaders often think that making people happy at work will build a better culture, but the truth is that if we want people to be happy at work, we need to help them get better at it.

▶ Examples

▶ Example #1

Mrs. Jensen, today when I was in your classroom observing, the primary instructional strategy that I saw was round-robin reading. We've spent a lot of time this school year on high leverage literacy strategies, specifically the Socratic Seminar. Unfortunately, round-robin reading is a surface-level strategy that can inadvertently create disengagement, interrupt the flow of the text, and potentially embarrass struggling readers. We've focused on the Socratic Seminar since it requires students to analyze a passage, think critically, identify key details, and make evidence-based interpretations. It also builds transferable reading skills. Imagine the amplified impact of the passage you were having students read about the teenager who was hospitalized due to vaping if they were working in small groups, analyzing the situation, and preparing to collaboratively discuss with classmates. For your next health lesson that requires reading, let's plan a 10-minute Socratic seminar together. I can model the structure and walk through the key aspects of the strategy and how to use it in class. Please schedule a time for us to meet.

The first two sentences of the feedback open the conversation and immediately identify what was observed: *The primary instructional strategy I saw was round-robin reading.* This eliminates any confusion and clearly puts the strategy as the focal point of the feedback. The next line establishes what the school instructional focus has been all year and the high leverage strategy learned: *We've spent a lot of time this school year on high leverage literacy strategies, specifically the Socratic Seminar.* The next couple of lines clearly note how to change the lesson by identifying the weakness of the one strategy compared to the other. It's important to provide a rationale and evidence backing your claim: *...round-robin reading inadvertently creates disengagement, interrupts the flow of the text, and potentially embarrass struggling readers. We've focused on the Socratic Seminar since it requires students to analyze a passage, think critically, identify key details, and make evidence-based interpretations.* The last few lines are vital for the feedback to make an impact since it offers clear support and next steps: *Let's plan a 10-minute Socratic Seminar together. I will model the structure and walk through the key aspects of the strategy and how to use it in class. Please schedule a time for us to meet.*

▶ *Example #2*

Mrs. Lowery, as I observed your lesson today, I noticed that some students were able to underline key phrases from the passage, and a few explained their choices to me. While it's important for learners to recognize main ideas, research shows that highlighting, by itself, is a surface-level strategy with a relatively low effect on comprehension and retention. To deepen students' understanding they need to also analyze, discuss, and apply what they've read. To take this lesson further, I'd like to see the highlighting strategy as the initial phase of the activity and then have students compare and contrast their highlighted sections in pairs. This fits right into the Think-Pair-Share strategy that we learned earlier this year. This will help ensure that your students aren't just identifying text but actually comprehending it. I'm attaching a Think-Pair-Share stem statement handout that can guide each aspect of the T-P-S strategy. Please let me know the next time you use this, I would love to pop in and see you in action again.

In Example 1, the teacher chose an inferior strategy, while in Example 2, she is simply not going far enough with a good strategy: *While it's important for learners to recognize main ideas, research shows that highlighting, by itself, is a surface-level strategy..."* Similar to Example 1, this Performance Coaching feedback details the other aspects of highlighting—comparing and contrasting the highlighted sections—that makes this a better and more complete reading strategy. Lastly, the instructional leader offers a strategy that can easily improve the lesson. Think-Pair-Share is relatively simple to implement, especially given the shared resource as support: *I'm attaching a Think-Pair-Share stem statement handout that can guide each aspect of the T-P-S strategy.* Also note that the observer is hinting at the fact that she will return "pop in" again, which increases the pressure to make the change by using the resource provided.

▶ Example #3

Mr. Lopez, when I visited your classroom today, I noticed that students were solving a set of computation problems independently for 27 minutes. While this provides practice, research shows that rote repetition alone has a limited effect on deep learning. To deepen understanding, try a short Number Talk. This will require students to explain the different ways they solved a problem and force them to back up their rationale. As you know, Number Talks, done well, builds number sense and flexibility. I'll share some sample prompts you can use to ensure that students go beyond answers and into mathematical thinking. Let me know if you have any questions.

For this example, you will see that the feedback is more direct and doesn't go into great detail. You know your teachers best and you can tailor the feedback so it is "heard" by the teacher. This feedback doesn't deviate from the formula; it just explicitly states how to deepen the learning, similar to the other examples. There are a few important nuances that you can identify: (1) The "27 minutes" of independent practice is entirely objective, not based on preference or opinion, (2) The observer clearly believes that the teacher can do a Number Talk to improve lesson structure with only the sample prompts available, and (3) The rationale alone is enough to motivate the teacher. This is all based on your knowledge of each staff member, their willingness to change, and your follow-up to observe again with frequency in mind.

▶ *Example #4*

Coach Davis, during my walkthrough today, I saw you demonstrate a few fundamental basketball skills, such as dribbling and passing, but then the students were divided up and given time to shoot around for the remaining 25 minutes. While the students played and seemed to enjoy themselves, the open court play doesn't give them ample time to learn the skills. To ensure that they're learning the fundamentals of the game, I'd like you to add a few station-based activities, such as passing, layup drills, and defensive movements. This balances the fun with targeted skill-building. I can share sample station cards to make setup easy if needed. Let me know. Otherwise, I'll check back next week to see the difference, even if you've moved on to another sport in the sequence or the curriculum.

For the last example, you can identify the parts of the model on your own. What we want to double down on is that the observer always identifies what they saw and how it can be improved. There are no generalities, and the feedback gets right to the point. We emphasize this because as the lead learner, you are always building and developing a culture of excellence, including the support needed to make changes incrementally and with speed. That's the path to overall school improvement. The feedback and the support demonstrate candor and care that will elevate everyone's abilities toward student growth. The only other thing to point out here is that the final sentence is a nod toward the fact that the teacher is expected to apply the instructional change to the lessons, regardless of the content, and that there will, in fact, be another visit for accountability with that.

▶ **CONCLUSION**

While Lara was terrific at giving Specific Praise, her Performance Coaching feedback was lacking, creating a culture of stagnation, and, at times, regression. Building a feedback-rich culture that thrives on continuous improvement is challenging, but it's also a very rewarding aspect of leadership. While growth is difficult and change is hard, the four-part Performance Coaching feedback model creates a structure to guide conversations, elevate research- and evidence-based best practices, and focus relentlessly on getting better.

As Yoda reminds Lara, true coaching, delivered with precision on *what to change* and *how to change*, within a supportive environment, is a gift. As Lara develops this skill, she will improve her teachers' instructional practices and move the school closer toward its goals. The process will not be easy at first; the traps are real and mastering the four-part model will take time.

Either way, she needs to show herself some grace as she implements this tactic. Just as we are developing teachers to become their best self, we need to remind ourselves that leadership is a developmental process as well. As Yoda reminds Lara, mastery comes with time, but clear expectations, high standards, and accountability are nothing to be ashamed of.

▶ Next Steps Checklist

- Conduct classroom visits with curiosity. As you look for bright spots for praise, also consider areas that need improvement. What are your teachers' practices that need to be strengthened or changed?
- When you're in a classroom and you identify an area of need, categorize it into one of three primary areas: classroom culture, the curriculum, and the instructional focus of the school or district.
- Use your four-part model—what to change, why to change it, how to change it, and provide support.
- Be sure to check your four-part model to ensure that you used all four parts at least once each and in the right order.
- Send the message, leave the note, or log the performance coaching feedback in your system. Hold yourself accountable by providing the feedback before you leave the room.

Improving Conversations

6

▶ TIM'S QUESTIONS ARE CONDESCENDING

Tim celebrates his teachers regularly, and he moves the needle when it comes to instructional practices. Unlike Lara, Tim has most of the instructional leadership equation down, including performance coaching for improved results at the classroom level. The problem is that Tim is trying to use questions to empower and engage his teachers in a reflective practice, rather than dictating their work, but his questions are too broad and indirect, which come off more performative than supportive. Tim wants his teachers to be thoughtful and reflective; however, his questions are crafted in a way that makes his teachers feel like they're trying to guess what he's thinking rather than trying to understand more about what they're thinking.

Tim has an extensive instructional background. He was a lead learner for his department when he taught, then was promoted to an instructional coach at the district office. After a couple of years, he became an academic dean, then an assistant principal in charge of pathways and AP coursework, all before becoming a principal. He's in his third year as the principal of Pliny Middle School, and the school has noticed marked improvement on the end-of-course exams and the state test scores. Most of their success is due to an increased focus on research-based instructional practice and effective implementation. The teachers have come to welcome Tim's feedback on their practices because he doesn't miss an opportunity to praise their work and his coaching directives are clear and reasonable.

The trouble is that Tim wants to move more into deep conversations with his teachers rather than just celebrating what they do well and telling them what and how to change where they fall short. He wants to coach them more and have them become better reflective practitioners. He read a few coaching books that emphasized the power of questioning as an important aspect of helping people grow, especially if we want them to grow on their own. The issue is how Tim phrases his questions. They don't invite dialogue or express curiosity; instead, his questions sound more like he's trying to control the conversation, making assumptions about what teachers think about their own practices, rather than inviting dialogue. This is now beginning to undermine the qualities and traits that the teachers have come to respect and value in Tim as their principal.

The frustration is mounting because they would rather Tim just tell them what to do than use this new approach with dialogue. They're not wrong. Tim's questions are problematic for two reasons: they're worded in a way that either baits the teachers into coming to the same realization that he already has or lures them into the realization that they did something wrong. If he doesn't change this approach soon, he's going to lose the staff.

Fortunately for Tim, Yoda is available and has the ability to help him use the same enthusiasm that made him an instructional powerhouse to become a high-level questioner. Yoda knows he has to help Tim see that questions are about curiosity and common understanding, not about fixing people, exacting judgment, or confirming his own bias.

▶ YOUR QUESTIONS ARE FRUSTRATING THE TEACHERS

Tim's questioning strategy frustrates the teachers. They would prefer that he sticks with telling them what he wants them to do differently, which at least is direct and clear. But, Tim knows that an empowered staff, skilled in professional dialogue and problem-solving techniques, will enable the school to achieve even greater success. Specific Praise and Performance Coaching are great communication skills for the leader to have, but they are only two-thirds of the equation. When scaling an environment of continuous improvement, developing leading learners is essential and requires a focused interchange of ideas where people freely question, challenge, and support one another. That's the culture that Tim is trying to build, but he's falling into three very common traps that plague school leaders who aren't trained in how to approach questioning from a position of curiosity versus certainty.

▶ Trap #1: Asking Leading Questions

Leading questions are naturally judgmental, assumptive, and directive. They are worded in a way that suggests that there's already a right answer that the questioner knows the answer to and the respondent needs to formulate. A leading question comes into play when the person asking the question is doing one of two things: (1) They're trying to lure the person being questioned into understanding something that the questioner already knows the answer to. (2) They're leading someone into the realization that they did something incorrect that needs to be fixed.

One of the biggest problems with leading questions is that the person on the receiving end is put in a defensive position. They're trapped trying to guess what the questioner is thinking or contemplating that they did wrong. This creates a power struggle rather than a conversation. The goal of professional dialogue is to elevate the expertise of the person being asked the questions. Leading questions do the opposite, creating stagnation or, worse yet, regression. They should be avoided entirely.

One antidote to asking leading questions is to use Performance Coaching instead. School leaders often feel the urge to "lead" teachers toward making different decisions about instructional practices through questioning. This is no different than when teachers "funnel" students to an answer through narrow and leading questions to arrive at a predetermined answer.

Leaders must harness the power of an observation, which enables them to assess, analyze, reflect, and understand the work being done by the teacher. Regardless of the supervisory role or positions of power, the person doing the observing has a distinct advantage in knowing the tweaks and modifications that should be made to improve the person's performance. It's critical to simply point this out what needs to change, through Performance Coaching, rather than trying to use questions that direct them to the tweaks and modifications that we're already aware of.

To further the problem, we've unfortunately witnessed training modules and professional development that actually teaches school leaders that questions of this kind can help teachers to become reflective practitioners. That couldn't be further from the truth. This type of false guidance is not grounded in research and mostly anecdotal, based entirely on someone's experience as an instructional coach or school leader and not behavioral psychology or neuroscience. The point of leading learning and the practices associated with instructional leadership is to celebrate what works, direct the work of making incremental progress, instill a sense of curiosity through dialogue, and strengthen self-awareness and metacognition. When you want someone to know what you're thinking, just tell them; don't mask your opinion through questioning.

▶ *Trap #2: Having All the Answers and Fixing Problems for Others*

The second trap in asking poorly constructed questions is when leaders believe that they have all the answers and need to use those answers to fix everyone else's problems. We call this the Fix-It Fallacy. School leaders fall into this trap because they're altruistic and want to help. But, in an effort to support people, we provide them with answers and solutions, which creates a situation where we are back to asking leading questions. The truth is that a single person cannot solve a school's problems, and although school leaders need to be instructionally focused, they don't have to know all the answers nor do they have to fix all the problems on their own.

This is a mindset shift in the approach to leading learning. As we'll discuss further, it's sometimes better to be open and candid about being unclear on the path forward than to position yourself as the only person who can solve the school's problems. This is especially true when it comes to all of the teachers' classroom practices. It's somewhat understandable how leaders can easily fall into this trap because the sheer nature of naming the principal as the "instructional leader," seems to put all of the onus of the instruction on their shoulders. Although it becomes their obligation to improve instructional practices, it can't be their sole responsibility to do so. This changes the types of questions we ask from leading to exploratory.

Another pitfall within this trap is trying to move too quickly. Knowing all the answers and fixing all the problems might appear to be the fastest way to improve outcomes, but it's not feasible, not sustainable, and most of all overlooks the incredible contributions that the team can provide.

Using professional dialogue appropriately builds a culture where everyone takes ownership of solving the school's problems and improving classroom practices. A principal, acting as an instructional leader, sets the tone for this to take place but doesn't make it their job to have the answer to every scenario. Asking better questions changes the environment and the mentality of the people who work within it toward a culture of inquisition, examination, and experimentation.

▶ Trap #3: Confirming Your Own Bias

The third trap frustrates people to no end. This is when leaders ask questions to confirm their own bias regarding a practice, situation, or strategy. This only promotes the status quo, fosters defensiveness, and impedes trust. In fact, in the case of confirmation bias, the teacher you're attempting to influence will only regress toward a general system of beliefs that everyone holds. It could be a good thing if we all subscribe to the same expert practices, but if those beliefs are inaccurate, we'll never make progress. There are plenty of private and public enterprises where confirmation bias was precisely what led the organization to its demise. The leadership at Blockbuster, for example, stayed steadfast to their brick-and-mortar model along with short-term profits despite the changing landscape, including new technology and other information that challenged their long-held assumptions about the market. Eventually, they failed.

Quality questions should be about introspection not confirmation. Had Blockbuster asked open-ended questions of their employees and customers, they would have learned quickly that they needed a long-range plan to succeed. Going back to Tim from the beginning of the chapter, his questions are meant to control what people think, not expand their minds (or his for that matter). We don't need people to tell us what *we're thinking*; we need them to share what *they're thinking*. And, we want them to stretch beyond what they currently think through curiosity, self-analysis, and dialogue.

When coaching people, we want to use questions that lead to a common understanding. This may be regarding a process that's not entirely clear to the coach, a desire to understand someone's thinking and choice of strategies, or their motivation and vision. Quality questions should lead to one of two outcomes: (1) The instructional leader's ability to provide more Specific Praise or Performance Coaching or (2) The teachers ability to reflect in a way that they might not have without the question. We'll come back to both of these outcomes in the coming sections.

▶ ASKING BETTER QUESTIONS

The key to asking better questions and to avoiding the traps that we've discussed is for the leaders to literally shift their thinking from one of evaluator and manager to coach and growth partner. This begins with the leader starting from a place of curiosity. The concept of becoming a strong instructional leader has the potential to seemingly contradict curiosity because it's counterintuitive to "lead instruction" without being directive and having all the answers as to what the instruction should look like in practice. While we encourage school leaders to be well-versed in instruction—including the work of John Hattie, Robert Marzano, Richard DuFour, Charlotte Danielson, Zaretta Hammond, and others—we also know that instructional leadership is as much about culture building as it is about the know-how and expertise of the leader.

When we train leaders on our models for leading learning, we always start with specific praise then move on to performance coaching and, finally, professional dialogue third. It's not because one is more important than the other but rather how they progress in mastery of their use. In other words, understanding and using professional dialogue is the hardest of the three to master. We previously established that *we shouldn't use questions* to lure people into thinking something that we already know to be true or to bait them into believing that they did something wrong. It's time to discuss the reasons why and times when *we should use questions.*

The best questions for instructional leaders are designed to uncover something that we didn't see during the observation because of the natural flaws in the observation cycle or to reveal the thinking behind something that we did see and don't quite understand. Let's unpack this further. Any observation cycle—whether formal or informal—has inherent flaws due to the nature of the gaps in time before and after a visit and between observations. In other words, for short visits, such as walkthroughs, you miss what happened just before you entered the classroom or after you leave. Of course, if you're there for the beginning of the period of instruction, you only miss what happens after you leave and vice versa for when you see the end of a period of instruction. This is true at every level, regardless of self-contained elementary classrooms with blocks of instruction unfolding throughout the day or secondary schools where teachers have different groups of students moving through a set schedule. Hence, the flaw in not seeing what happens when you're not there and the formation of a good question about it.

The other type of question is about the thinking that goes into something that you did see. If a teacher, for example, allows a student to have their head down on the desk while you're in the room, without prompting that student to engage in the lesson, you likely have no idea why the teacher is permitting that behavior. Your reaction might be to ask the teacher to reengage students when they clearly aren't paying attention, but it's better to ask why they did that—what were they thinking when that took place. We'll come back to this in our examples.

▶ THE TACTIC: PROFESSIONAL DIALOGUE MODEL

Our model for coaching through the use of questions is called Professional Dialogue. Like the other models, we're very intentional about the naming convention and nomenclature. We use *professional* because we want to stay on task with the work, rather than veering into a rabbit-hole of personal banter about Sunday's football game. In *Candid and Compassionate Feedback* (2018) we dubbed that kind of leader as the *Easer Inner*—someone who spends 58 minutes of an hour-long meeting talking about nonsense and then 2 minutes trying to cover the important stuff. That might be a bit of an exaggeration, but you get the point.

We use the word *dialogue* to signify that there should be an exchange of ideas. One thing that you'll notice in the model for Professional Dialogue is that there's an emphasis on clarity—clarity about what you didn't see, clarity about what you want to know, clarity about what was shared, and clarity about the steps forward. The point of these professional exchanges is no different than the use of Specific Praise or Performance Coaching; we're working to reinforce and improve practice. In fact, you'll

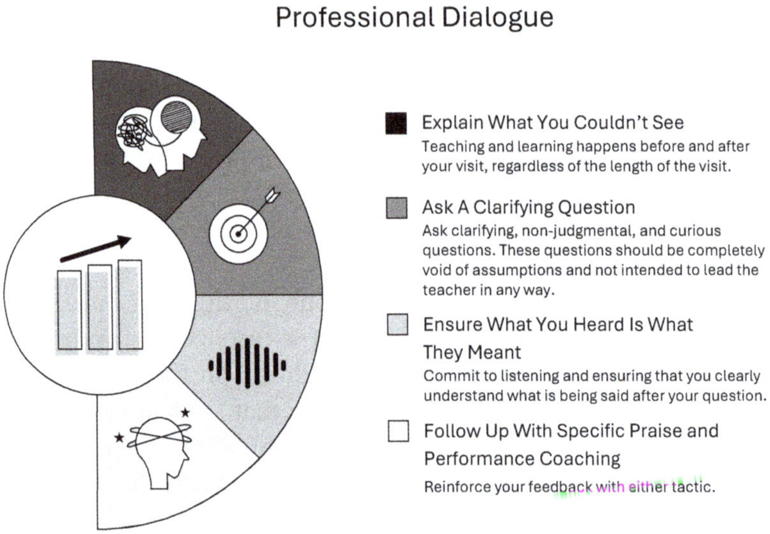

Professional Dialogue

- **Explain What You Couldn't See**
  Teaching and learning happens before and after your visit, regardless of the length of the visit.

- **Ask A Clarifying Question**
  Ask clarifying, non-judgmental, and curious questions. These questions should be completely void of assumptions and not intended to lead the teacher in any way.

- **Ensure What You Heard Is What They Meant**
  Commit to listening and ensuring that you clearly understand what is being said after your question.

- **Follow Up With Specific Praise and Performance Coaching**
  Reinforce your feedback with either tactic.

Figure 6.1 Professional Dialogue

see in the model below that your questions are leading you to celebrate or coach in every case (Figure 6.1).

▶ The Model

The Professional Dialogue model has four parts, and you'll learn how to use each part, why they're vital for successful conversations, and how to use each part appropriately and effectively. Let's dive into Part 1 of the model.

▶ Part 1: Explain What You Couldn't See

The first part of the Professional Dialogue model is to acknowledge that there is an inherent flaw in the observation cycle. As discussed previously, you can't observe all of what happens during instruction because you're not there every day all day like the teacher is. Teaching and learning happen before and after your visit, regardless of the length of the visit. Even if you stay the entire period, teaching and learning occurred the previous day and will ensue the next day, likely without you there. The Professional Dialogue is designed for successful and productive conversations, rather than assumptions about things that we can't see and minds that we can't read. As instructional leaders, vulnerability is important for trust. When we clarify from the beginning that there are obvious flaws in observing something as dynamic as teaching, it helps to relieve the pressure for both the leader and the teacher that they must have all the answers.

Another important aspect in explaining the flaw is that it prevents the natural tendency of a teacher to become defensive toward the observer because the intricacies and nuances of the job are acknowledged. Without the recognition that you miss things as an observer, whether you're there or not, you set your question up to fail because the most natural response for the teacher will be to believe that you're trying to find something that they did wrong. This can be as simple as opening your model with "I didn't get to see the closing activity you had on your agenda today..." and then asking the question in Part 2 of the model.

▶ *Part 2: Ask a Clarifying Question*

The second part of the Professional Dialogue model is to ask clarifying, non-judgmental, and curious questions. These questions should be completely void of assumptions and not intended to lead the teacher in any way. Remember, instructional leadership is as much about what your teachers know and the decisions they make as it is about what you know and want them to do. Now that you've primed them with the flaw in your observation, you're asking a quality question to clarify something of interest. It's at this point that we like to tell leaders that if you don't have a question, don't ask one. The minute you ask a question, you're requiring more work. Either through processing a verbal response or typing one up to reply, you're making the teacher think and respond, which is a good thing, but only when necessary.

When you ask a clarifying question, you want to know something about what you couldn't see or what the teacher was thinking when they did something when you were there or when they planned the lesson in the first place. Following up on Part 1, it might sound something like this: "How did you check for understanding during the lesson closure, and what did you learn from that?" Or "What closing strategies are you finding most helpful to gauge how well students are grasping this content?" If closing strategies, data collection, or exit tickets are clearly defined in your Principles of Instruction, reviewed as expectations during professional development, or previously discussed in a pre- or post-observation conference with this particular teacher, this is a perfectly positioned reflective, clarifying question.

▶ *Part 3: Ensure What You Heard Was What They Meant*

Part 3 of the Professional Dialogue model is a leadership lesson in itself. What people say and what they mean are often two different things, and what people say and what you hear are often worlds apart. Even when we listen to understand versus to respond, as Covey (1990) teaches in the famous *7 Habits of Highly Effective People*, we miss things and misinterpret things more easily than we realize. If we want the Professional

Dialogue model to work, we have to be clear on what the person says after we ask our question. Any assumption throughout the process is an immediate conversation-killer.

Suppose the teacher answers the question from Part 2 with "I didn't get to the closing strategy that was on the agenda" and leaves it at that. This requires further questioning. Suppose, instead, that they say,

> I used a 3-2-1 question as an exit ticket. Three things they learned today, 2 things that are still unclear, and 1 question that they want me to answer tomorrow. Many of the students had similar questions, which is going to guide my warm-up tomorrow.

You might then respond with "It sounds like you uncovered a key gap that you can fill through data collection on your exit tickets. Am I hearing that correctly?" If the teacher says "yes," you use Specific Praise in Part 4, especially if the exit ticket and data collection are instructional strategies that the school emphasizes. More examples to follow.

▶ *Part 4: Follow Up with Specific Praise or Performance Coaching*

Berger (2016) contends that one of the main reasons to ask better questions is to be able to praise or coach in response. That's exactly what our model for professional dialogue leads to in Part 4. The point of instructional leadership is school improvement, and the result of feedback should be to reinforce or change a practice, including the use of questioning. It means that feedback always leads to change. In the case of reinforcement, it guides the thinking of the receiver to do more of what we praise; that's a change in behavior. In the case of performance coaching, we're asking teachers to tweak a practice or do something different altogether.

Continuing with our response to the teacher's 3-2-1 exit ticket that included data collection, we would definitely want to use the Specific Praise model to reinforce what we clarified from the question. There are, of course, options. You have to decide which aspect of the practice is most important to reinforce, asking yourself the question: what do I most want this teacher to repeat? It's likely data collection, the use of an exit ticket, or something we recently learned in a professional development experience. Each of the examples below demonstrates some of the choices you might make as an instructional leader based on the variations of the responses from the teacher.

▶ *Examples*

▶ *Example #1*

Question: *I didn't get to see the closing activity you had on your agenda today; did you collect any data by using an exit ticket or another strategy to see how students are performing on this learning set?*

Answer: *I used a 3-2-1 question as an exit ticket. Three things they learned today, 2 things that are still unclear, and 1 question that they want me to answer tomorrow. Many of the students had similar questions, which is going to guide my warm-up tomorrow.*

Clarification: *It sounds like you uncovered a key gap that you can fill through data collection on your exit tickets. Am I hearing that correctly?*

Confirmation: *Yes*

Response: *Well done. Thank you for implementing the 3-2-1 strategy that we recently learned from our instruction coach at our faculty meeting. It's so important that we continue to grow by trying the strategies that we learn. I'm so glad that it worked to provide the data you need for the warm-up tomorrow.*

In this case, the question revealed that the teacher used a strategy that was recently reviewed at a faculty meeting by the instructional coach. We're reinforcing the use of the strategy that we want teachers to try in the weeks after the professional learning took place. The choice we made as an instructional leader is to praise for effort and strengthen a culture of professional learning and implementation as a result. As instructional leaders, we might also want to know which gap was uncovered and how the teacher plans to fill it, but the point here is to praise the use of the strategy that was recently modeled at the faculty meeting. In Example 2, you'll see a slightly different decision.

▶ Example #2

Question: *I didn't get to see the closing activity you had on your agenda today; did you collect any data by using an exit ticket or another strategy to see how students are performing on this learning set?*

Answer: *I used a 3-2-1 question as an exit ticket. Three things they learned today, 2 things that are still unclear, and 1 question that they want me to answer tomorrow. Many of the students had similar questions, which is going to guide my warm-up tomorrow.*

Clarification: *It sounds like you uncovered a key gap that you can fill through data collection on your exit tickets. Am I hearing that correctly?*

Confirmation: *Yes*

Response: *Nicely done. Having a closing strategy at the end of the lesson is so important to gauge what was learned. It means that we're focused on learning, not just teaching, which is why we wrote the* Exit Ticket *into our* Principles of Instruction. *Fantastic work with that.*

In this variation, we're reinforcing the use of the Principles of Instruction (PoI), which is also an A.F.A. strategy that we'll learn more about in Chapter 7. The question, again, reveals the use of the 3-2-1, which is an Exit Ticket. The teacher is using the PoI to guide lesson planning, and the change in behavior is to continue to do that versus deviating from it. It's amazing how quick people will discard a behavior if it's not reinforced with praise. Again, we also might be curious about the actual gaps, but the point is to reinforce the use of the PoI. The gaps can be revealed and discussed in PLCs.

▶ Example #3

Question: *I didn't get to see the closing activity you had on your agenda today; did you collect any data by using an exit ticket or another strategy to see how students are performing on this learning set?*

Answer: *I used a 3-2-1 question as an exit ticket. Three things they learned today, 2 things that are still unclear, and 1 question that they want me to answer tomorrow. Many of the students had similar questions, which is going to guide my warm-up tomorrow.*

Clarification: *It sounds like you uncovered a key gap that you can fill through data collection on your exit tickets. Am I hearing that correctly?*
Confirmation: *Yes*
Response: *Great work! Thank you for collecting data at the end of your lesson to demonstrate what students retained and what needs to be followed up on in subsequent lessons. I'm glad to hear that you're using this data for tomorrow's warm up. Without data, we have no idea if what we taught was actually retained. Well done and kudos to you.*

This time, we're reinforcing the use of data as the primary aspect of the lesson that we want the teacher to repeat. Maybe the school has a focus on PLCs and the data is reviewed by a team of teachers who will ask the traditional questions: What do we want students to learn? How will we know if they learned it? What will we do if they learn it? What will we do if they don't? (DuFour et al., 2010). This also means that we could just as easily praise the PLC structure as a fourth option. In Example 4, we'll take a look at what happens when the teacher fails to follow the agenda that included the Exit Strategy.

▶ *Example #4*

Question: *I didn't get to see the closing activity you had on your agenda today; did you collect any data by using an exit ticket or another strategy to see how students are performing on this learning set?*
Answer: *I lost track of time at the end of the lesson, and I didn't get to the* Exit Ticket *that I had planned.*
Clarification: *To be clear, you planned an* Exit Ticket, *which is one of our Principles of Instruction, but you just didn't get to it because time got away from you?*
Confirmation: *Yeah. A few other things ran over, and the bell rang before I knew it.*
Response: *We can't run out of time at the end of a lesson and miss the mark with one of the most important structures of the plan, which is the* Exit Ticket. *It's critical that we collect data regarding what students understand so that we can make decisions for future lesson plans. Next time, set timers for your activities so that you know how long each learning set should last to*

be able to get to the Exit Ticket *before the end of the period; you can adjust on the fly to ensure that you get to it each day. To help with it, I'm linking to an Edutopia article about the importance of closure and strategies for implementation.*

In this example, the question ended up disclosing that the teacher failed to use one of the Principles of Instruction because she lost track of time. Quality instruction is all about timing, and we want our teachers to master the minutes and seconds that they have with students. The instructional leader chooses to use our Performance Coaching model to change this scenario for the future, and the teacher should feel both the pressure and support to make the change moving forward.

> ### LEADER WELL-BEING SIDE NOTE: BE FLEXIBLE—REMAIN FLEXIBLE IN THE APPROACH AND STEADFAST IN THE OUTCOMES
>
> Many leaders worry that if the work doesn't get done exactly the way that they would do it, it won't be good enough. Asking better questions and being curious also means that you have to accept valid ideas that others have and be less rigid. This is freeing for the leader and empowering for others. You can be flexible in how your teachers respond and with the ideas that they share while still being steadfast in obtaining the results.
>
> For example, suppose one of your Principles of Instruction is an Exit Ticket. The 3-2-1 is one of many good strategies, but there are plenty of other closing strategies that work. You should set very clear expectations that a closing strategy should be used at the end of every lesson. When the second-grade reading lesson ends, a closing strategy is expected. When the fifth-grade math lesson ends, a closing strategy is expected. Before the end of the ninth-grade science period comes to a close, you expect some sort of Exit Ticket.
>
> But, the way that the teacher designs the closure is flexible and not as rigid as a 3-2-1 every time. As an instructional leader, you don't want to control every aspect of every lesson; it's better to simply establish clear expectations pertaining to instructional excellence. Empower your teachers, set boundaries, and free yourself from the decision-making process that goes into the details of a lesson plan. When the Principles of Instruction are alive and well, you're mostly getting out of the way and spending your time celebrating success.

▶ CONCLUSION

It's important to remember that asking better questions is about improving conversations. Improving conversations is about thoughtful professional dialogue. Dialogue is a two-way exchange that results in clarity, introspection, reflection, and change. You're never trying to bait people into thinking what you already know to be true, guess what you're thinking, or come to the conclusion that they did something wrong. You're using conversations as a tactic to build a culture where we question what works, think about our thinking, and rely on a strong rationale for our decisions. Even if you have a very set and scripted curriculum, we still want teachers to think hard about their actions and behaviors as they implement the curriculum. There should never be a time when teachers aren't thoughtful about their work, and asking better questions helps with that.

Lastly, if you don't have an important question to ask, don't ask one. Now that we've reviewed all three models as tactics for instructional leadership, it's critical that you understand the degree to which each should be used. The proportions are not necessarily equal. We use Specific Praise all of the time; Performance Coaching some of the time; and Professional Dialogue sparingly. Specific Praise is our default tactic since it lifts people, sets the tone for a positive culture, and reinforces effective practice. The bottom line is that you can't use it enough. Performance Coaching is used to address challenges and stretch our teacher's performance. Professional Dialogue promotes reflection and metacognition. Professional Dialogue offers broader perspectives and the sharing of insights. This requires the greatest cognitive load of the three, and should not be a burden to a teacher unless sparked by your genuine curiosity as the leader of learning.

As Tim continues to work with Yoda, his skill set in asking better questions grows and his teachers are having a better experience. Not only does he get a really thoughtful response from his teachers, the culture is changing in the way he intended. He quits leading his teachers toward what he's thinking, and he phrases his questions in a way that values what they're thinking. Better questions result in better dialogue, and better dialogue results in reflection and improvements to classroom practices.

That's instructional leadership from a principal who is truly leading learning.

▶ Next Steps Checklist

- Be curious when you visit the most important spaces in your school—the classroom.
- Ask questions about things you can't see, such as what happened before or after you leave and the decision that teachers make when they plan.
- Avoid leading questions, fixing every problem yourself, and confirmation bias. You want to empower your teachers to make quality instructional decisions on their own.
- Use the Professional Dialogue four-part model that ends with Specific Praise or Performance Coaching. Instructional leadership is always about school improvement, reinforcing what works and changing what doesn't.
- Don't use Professional Dialogue unnecessarily. It places a cognitive demand on teachers to think and respond thoughtfully. That's a good thing but only when the situation calls for it.

References

Berger, W. (2016). *A more beautiful question: The power of inquiry to spark breakthrough ideas.* London: Bloomsbury.

Covey, S. R. (1990). *7 habits of highly effective people: Powerful lessons in personal change.* New York: Simon and Schuster.

DuFour, R., DuFour, R., Eaker, R., Many, T. W., Mattos, M., & Muhammad, A. (2024). *Learning by doing: A handbook for professional learning communities at work* (4th ed.). Bloomington, IN: Solution Tree Press.

Jones, J., & Vari, T. (2018). *Candid and compassionate feedback: Transforming everyday practice in schools.* New York: Routledge.

Part 3

Systems for Managing Change

Anchoring, Focusing, and Aligning the Work

▶ LARISA'S FEEDBACK ISN'T COHERENT

Larisa is in her fifth year as principal and fully believes she is starting to hit her stride as a leader. She felt it toward the end of the last school year when there was a noticeable shift within herself and her staff—she was no longer trying to prove herself, her confidence was high, and she was consistently identifying the possibilities at Maple Ridge Middle School.

As a strong leader, she excels at praising her staff, she doesn't duck tough conversations, and willingly engages in dialogue as a coach. She has worked hard on each of the tactics for instructional leadership, especially her questioning techniques to elicit deep reflection and analysis from her teachers. There is a glitch though. Amid all her strengths, her feedback can still feel like individual puzzle pieces, scattered on a table for her teachers to assemble. Each piece of her communication is strong, even valuable, just not aligned and tied to the bigger picture. To her staff, her feedback is meaningful, but it's not linked to a greater purpose.

Over the last couple of years, Larisa and her teachers have worked hard to identify the overarching framework for teaching and learning. They have clear instructional priorities, a comprehensive learning guide that aligns the standards to the curriculum, a purposeful professional learning plan, a detailed assessment framework, and collaborative structures that allow teachers to learn and grow together. The work they've accomplished is nothing short of impressive. Oddly, though, Larisa's feedback lacks coherence with the framework. Her feedback isn't wrong, it just doesn't clearly tie back to the overall focus, which creates confusion and leaves teachers uncertain about what really matters.

Teachers at Maple Ridge want to improve and they are eager to grow and learn, but the feedback they are receiving is not helping them. Instead, it's causing frustration and even resentment. They've spent a significant amount of time and energy on developing and mastering the teaching and learning framework, while studying research and creating lessons. The staff is fully committed to making it work, much to the credit of Larisa.

The problem became clear after a walkthrough in a teacher leader's classroom. Larisa was in a room and the teacher was using a newly learned student discourse strategy called Save The Last Word For Me. In groups of four, students had to read various excerpts from Dr. King's Letter from Birmingham Jail and complete the activity as outlined. The teacher even added excellent prompts, such as "How does King justify breaking certain laws while respecting others?"

The teacher was excited to talk to Larisa about what she observed, but was taken back when the conversation wasn't on student discourse, but on technology. Larisa explained, "Next time, have students record their discussions on Flip so that you can capture their voices." The teacher was noticeably perplexed and disappointed. Larisa noticed the look on her teacher's face, but decided not to ask about it. Larisa didn't make it this far on her own; she is blessed to work with the district's executive coach. Yoda has been coaching her for three years and has helped her master the essential feedback techniques. During her most recent session, Larisa shared with Yoda her encounter with the teacher leader and his puzzled reaction to her feedback.

Yoda, a master coach, listened intently and then asked, "it doesn't sound like that feedback is directly connected to your school's instructional focus on student discourse." *Larisa thought about the last few walkthroughs that she conducted and even went back to a few emails that she sent her teachers. The answer was clear—it wasn't. Her feedback was good, even tied to good teaching practices, just not Maple Ridges' priorities. Yoda smiled and calmly expressed,* "feedback without alignment and coherence is like a compass that doesn't give direction. Teachers can't build on feedback that isn't anchored, focused, and aligned."

Larisa was frustrated with herself, but Yoda redirected her attention from what she was doing to what she was going to start doing. "From now on, Larisa, you're a coherence builder. Specific Praise, Performance Coaching, and Professional Dialogue will be clearly anchored, focused, and aligned to your school's teaching and learning framework." *Larisa felt slightly embarrassed. All of her team's hard work and she was plowing forward with new ideas and random suggestions. She made a commitment right then and there that her school's priorities would always be the backbone of her feedback.*

▶ YOUR FEEDBACK ISN'T SYSTEMATIC

Larisa's situation is not unique. She's a gifted leader focused on improving her teachers' instructional practices and working toward stronger student outcomes. This mindset is a forward-thinking, aggressive approach to moving the school to success. The challenge is that it can also continue to search for the next best thing as the answer to their problems. Unfortunately, the result is that the feedback, a key driver of improvement, does not support the overall goals in a deliberate and methodical fashion. What perplexes many leaders is that the feedback is still good and even accurate advice, but because it's not targeted and aligned to the priorities, it obscures the focus and dilutes the impact. Teachers may improve in some ways or in certain methods, but it doesn't spark a concerted movement for all teachers in unison.

The results are staggering—growth becomes fragmented, momentum stalls, and coherence quickly unravels. As Fullan and Quinn (2016) posit, without clarity and focus, even the most innovative practices can fail to create system-wide improvements. Coherence requires actionable shared meaning and purpose. To understand how to create those actions, we first want to dive into the three traps that ensnare even the best leaders, preventing them from providing anchored, focused, and aligned feedback.

▶ Trap #1: Providing Feedback That Isn't Anchored (Coherence) in the Vision of the School

One of the most prevalent traps that leaders experience is failing to anchor their feedback to the strategic priorities of the school, which should be grounded in the vision and mission. There are several reasons for this, but we find that there are two prominent causes: First, the leader has yet to fully internalize the key priorities that were identified and agreed upon. This may sound odd, but strategic planning itself is just an activity—an event that took place and lives on paper, yet not in the hearts and minds of the staff or even the leader.

Once the plan is written, the real work begins. Unfortunately, this is where many teams stop. It's not much different than how a blueprint functions in relation to a house. The blueprint captures the design, but the house still needs to get built. In the same way, a strategic plan is brought to life when the leader creates activities that enable people to understand the tenets of the plan, enact their role in achieving the goals, and weave the plan into the school's culture.

The second predominant reason is that leaders fall prey to what's referred to as the *shiny object syndrome*. They chase new ideas, practices, and strategies that are enticing but that are not anchored to the vision. This lack of focus creates an initiative overload where endless ideas and efforts pile up on top of one another without a clear throughline. Even the most talented leaders are susceptible to this because they want their teachers to be exceptional and their students to succeed. Their excitement over something they learned at a conference or read in the latest education journal lures them into believing that the new idea is the next "great" strategy. The reality is that school success takes time, which is not something that all school leaders have, leading them to jump from practice to practice without prioritizing with the hopes that something gives them the boost in student achievement that they're looking for.

Unfortunately, shiny object syndrome is a trap that perpetuates scattered ideas and disbanded priorities, leaving great strategies on the table yet never actuated in practice. Frustration mounts and the school leader jeopardizes the trust of their team. The antidote is to anchor as much of our feedback in the vision so that people have a clear north star, but we also need to focus on incremental progress rather than expecting massive changes to occur overnight.

▶ Trap #2: Providing Feedback That Isn't Focused (Momentum) on Incremental Improvements

A second trap that plagues leaders is the unrealistic expectation that huge successes will happen in the short term. Similar to not anchoring feedback in the vision, the leader is not making connections between what teachers are learning and the incremental progress that they're making in the classroom. As we've discussed throughout this book, delivering clear, actionable feedback is a skill. One of the more nuanced skills is to observe a teacher, provide Performance Coaching, return to see the tweaks in action, and note that the teacher has made progress.

The problem is that too many leaders don't realize that momentum occurs through smaller milestones. Teachers don't always recognize their own success when they take small steps in trying something new or different. Great leaders of learning celebrate even the tiniest change in practice to reinforce improvements little-by-little. We strengthen our teachers through reps and consistent feedback tied to the small changes that they're making.

We cannot overlook the importance of incremental progress because, when we add them all up, they act as a steady force for growth without completely overwhelming the teacher. Done well over time, the pacing of this type of feedback allows teachers to build toward larger goals, which they internalize, making mini-steps and using strategies that are necessary for actuating major gains.

▶ Trap #3: Providing Feedback That Isn't Aligned (Fragmented) to Professional Development

Another common trap is providing feedback that isn't connected to the professional development (PD) that teachers are receiving. This misstep is particularly damaging for a couple reasons. The PD provided throughout the school year should directly correspond with the goals and instructional priorities of the school. Essentially, drawing a throughline that connects the goals, the priorities, the associated activities, and then the intentional professional learning designed to equip the teachers with the skills necessary to achieve them. When feedback doesn't connect to what teachers are learning, the professional development is fragmented and devalued.

This sends mixed messages to staff on what is and is not important. While PD is offered to staff to learn and grow, the leader should be calculating how subsequent walkthrough feedback can be aligned to the new practices to solidify what is being learned. Think back to the feedback that Larisa gave to the teacher leader regarding the students' use of the Flip technology versus the teacher's use of a student discourse strategy (the latter being the school's instructional focus). It's easy to become frustrated and confused when the feedback isn't directly aligned to the PD, and, worse yet, when the feedback points to a strategy like technology, which actually prevents students from discourse.

Professional development is the internal source to drive instructional improvement in a school. Once teachers learn something new, school leaders should have plans in place to see the PD in action as quickly as possible. Not only is the feedback important after a PD to ensure that teachers are implementing, the visits are also opportunities to determine what supports and resources the teachers still may need. If we truly value PD, then the time spent after a session should be devoted to the teacher mastering their learning through ongoing feedback aligned to it.

▶ CULTIVATING COHERENCE

To fully embody the role of lead learner, school leaders must avoid the traps and intentionally cultivate coherence so that every effort drives momentum and progress. We've learned that school coherence is the key to success because without it, Specific Praise, Performance Coaching, and Professional Dialogue are less significant leaving teachers frustrated and unclear about what matters most. A school that lacks clarity crushes morale, and if the lead learner is unable to provide clear direction through supportive structures and coherent feedback, then stagnation and inertia are inevitable.

Achieving coherence means that there's a throughline that links the vision, mission, priorities, professional learning, and feedback so that they all work in harmony. This requires the leader to zoom out, embrace the big picture, and see how each aspect of instruction connects, like stars forming a constellation. Obscurity produces fragmented results. Fragmented results lead to frustration and disillusionment.

This is why the leader must embrace their role as the chief navigator to ensure coherence within the system. They are the sole individual who can breathe life into the priorities by consistently supporting them through anchored, focused, and aligned feedback. Effective school leaders don't just remind teachers of what matters. They demonstrate it through their actions.

The leader continually demonstrates what matters most time-and-time again, checking on teachers, determining their progress, praising their growth, and having dialogue about the work. Coherence brings everything into formation, which is necessary for a productive and successful environment for both students and teachers.

The most critical piece of coherence is impact. When everything is functioning in harmony, it's easier for the leader to determine what is and is not working. There are so many variables within a school that impact student success that aren't necessarily within the school's control. However, a coherent instructional framework supported through high-level professional development, clear actionable feedback, and ongoing monitoring is within the school's control and is also the responsibility of anyone who supervises teachers. This is the unified driver that leads to sustained school improvement.

Building coherence and staying on track, though, is no easy feat. Within any school or district, there are typically several competing initiatives that occupy space and crowd the same lane. The congestion creates bottlenecks and, at times, even collisions. The solution we offer is a practical tool called, A.F.A., which is the leader's guide to ensure coherence with instructional priorities and meaning feedback that is anchored, focused, and aligned to them.

▶ The Tool: A.F.A

Creating coherence begins with the school leader embracing their role as chief navigator. Their ability to step back and zoom out requires them to have an effective strategy to ensure coherence. A.F.A. is an acronym that serves as a defining reminder to anchor feedback to the vision, focus on incremental improvement, and align everything to professional development.

A.F.A. enables leaders to quickly evaluate every instructional initiative, effort, and decision through a clear lens. Remember, if there is too much congestion, we dilute our focus, which weakens our results. A.F.A. is a filter—a thinking process—to make certain that our feedback always revisits our priorities in a way that shows that they complement one another to make progress toward predetermined goals and outcomes (Figure 7.1).

▶ The Model

A.F.A. (Anchor, Focus, and Align) is a three-part framework that's designed to reinforce coherence within every aspect of

A.F.A.

A.F.A. optimizes performance and maximizes impact by ensuring that there is a through line woven among all the initiatives and activities to ensure they support and compliment one another.

1. Anchor to the Vision
By establishing the anchor, school leaders create the reference point that helps you maintain focus and remain steady on your goals.

2. Focus on Incremental Progress
Once the anchor is established, focus involves prioritizing tasks and responsibilities, so efforts are aligned to the anchor.

3. Align to Professional Learning
Alignment refers to all aspects of the work, the actions, strategies, resources, and people, are coordinated in a cohesive manner.

Figure 7.1 A.F.A.

instruction. Together, these three elements provide the tool to be used for instructional growth and success.

▶ Anchoring the Vision

Anchor grounds feedback so that it directly supports the vision and mission. One common problem associated with a school's vision and mission statements is that they don't permeate the school's culture through consistent decision-making. A vision statement needs to be connected to the daily priorities and day-to-day activities. This is how a vision lives within the school. We can't achieve the vision that we desire if our daily practices aren't aligned to it. Feedback that is anchored well creates the roadmap necessary for achievement. Anchoring also helps to assess whether or not the vision is crafted well. If it is too challenging to anchor the feedback to the vision, the vision should be revisited so that it's actionable. Vision statements are often too vague and abstract. A vision needs to clearly direct people in a way that they know what they need to do to advance the school. When vision statements point to excellence and achievement, as many do, so should our feedback when we're working with teachers. In this way, the teachers are always working to enact the vision, and our feedback should support that.

▶ Focusing on Incremental Change

Focus intensifies our attention on the growth of our teachers in a way that isn't always perceptible if we're not looking for it. It's a calculated approach to teacher development that builds incrementally over time and creates lasting change without overwhelming teachers. Of course, we want to see students achieve as quickly as possible, but improvements to instruction don't happen overnight. Teacher growth occurs like strokes on a canvas, and instructional leaders help to provide color and design. The work of an artist—any lead learner or any caring teacher—is never truly done. But, we must recognize the small wins and celebrate incremental growth on our journey toward excellence. One key to using the *Focus* tool is to remind teachers that they're better today than they were yesterday because they're following through on Specific Praise, Performance Coaching, and Professional Dialogue.

▶ *Aligning to Professional Development*

Align provides the guardrails so that the key drivers of our instructional framework are reinforced and moving in the right direction. If professional development is the engine for teacher growth, then that learning must be observed, supported, and refined through daily practice. This reframes how school leaders approach walkthroughs and observations. There is no time for random pop-ins so a leader can check a box. Instead, high achieving schools conduct frequent classroom visits that specifically look for mastery on the agreed upon priorities.

Any professional development (PD) day or event—such as days without students, faculty meetings, or PLCs—is the start of the race, not the end of it. Sitting through a PD that introduces new practices requires teachers to then use the strategies and receive feedback on how well they implement. The PD event is the intersection of growth for the teacher and the school leader. We contend that after any PD, an administrator should race to classrooms, eager to see how well the new learning is being delivered. If it is important enough to learn, then it's important to support. If the learning is grounded in what we want the teachers to change, we have to see them make that change as quickly after the PD occurs as possible. Aligned feedback closes the gap between theory and practice, learning and doing.

▶ **Examples**

▶ *Example #1: Praise with an Emphasis on Focus of A.F.A.*

Mrs. Hayes, I appreciate the opportunity to be in your class today. Last week, you took definite steps toward increasing student voice in your classroom by letting students know that you weren't going to just ask a single question and then just have one or two students respond. You told them your goal, which is also the school's goal, to engage students in more discussion and dialogue. You even took it a step further by framing what student discourse is, what it should look like in a class, and how it is a way for students to learn with and from each other.

Today, I noticed that you reinforced that expectation and then explicitly prompted students to listen, respond, and build on each other's ideas. I thought of the prompt you used a few times, "who can add to what Maya (or whichever student) said?" This is a simple way to intentionally create dialogue. Most importantly, though, six students raised their hands and were able to respond. You've set the expectation, created clear dialogue prompts, and held students accountable to respond. You've made several improvements to instruction based on our school goals, which is fantastic to see. Very well done.

The first two sentences of the feedback acknowledge that the observer has seen a change in the teacher's practice, even if it's small. It's also a side note about the walkthrough frequency and that the observer is seeing things over time. The teacher established how she was going to change her questioning technique, including why she was making that change. This helps with the context of the feedback and sets up the next few sentences, which identify the incremental progress that the teacher is making, which is the *Focus* part of A.F.A.

The feedback points out the iteration of what was observed, which was question prompts that created more student discourse than in the past: *I thought of the prompt you used a few times, with one example being 'who can add to what Maya said? This is a simple way to intentionally create dialogue.* It's important to note that this feedback is also an example of *Specific Praise* with *Focus* from A.F.A. as the teacher is incrementally improving how she is creating student discourse in her class. The final sentence adds a detail that also clearly demonstrates how the teacher is making changes to support the goals of the school. Evidence and examples are crucial for teacher reflection and continual growth: *Most importantly, though, six students raised their hands and were able to respond. You've set the expectation, created clear dialogue prompts, and held students accountable to respond.* This is clearly both new and different than past visits.

▶ *Example #2: Performance Coaching with an Emphasis on Anchor of A.F.A.*

Mrs. Banika, During the time I was in your class, you asked six questions. Each question followed the typical Initiate-Respond-Evaluate (IRE) framework. As you know, we are moving away from this style of questioning. You'll recall that IRE—when the teacher asks a question, a student gives a short answer, and the teacher confirms or corrects the response—trains students to give quick, low-level responses rather than to develop reasoning, elaborate ideas, or challenge one another.

In the future, please use a different method, such as Initiate-Respond-Probe, which still requires you to initiate the first question to garner students' initial responses, but rather than a simple answers, such as, "yes, that's right" or "no, that's not quite right," IRP requires you to probe the response and go deeper into the content. As we've discussed this year, student discourse is a key priority within our literacy plan.

Please let me know a good time to observe this technique. In the meantime, please use the attached resource to learn more about I-R-P.

In the first example, the teacher was using questioning prompts that were taught during PD and it was obvious to Larisa that she was progressively using the strategy in her class. In example 2, Mrs. Banika is still using the old method of questioning which is inferior. The feedback is specific: *During the time I was in your class, you asked six questions. Each question followed the typical Initiate-Respond-Evaluate (IRE) framework. As you know, we are moving away from this style of questioning* using Performance Coaching as the tactic. The next part of the feedback clearly describes a new technique: *In the future, please use a different method, such as Initiate-Respond-Probe…* so the teacher is clear on what is expected. The feedback then reiterates that this is a key priority for the school. Hence, the feedback is anchored to the vision:…*student discourse is a key priority within our literacy plan.*

As previously mentioned, Performance Coaching is not always received well. Anchoring the feedback to the vision and key priorities removes the subjectivity from the feedback and clearly identifies where the coaching suggestion is coming from.

It's not random or fragmented from what the teacher knows about the literacy goals for the school year, and the Performance Coaching is bordering on IDEAS, which we'll discuss in the next chapter.

▶ *Example #3: Specific Praise with an Emphasis on Anchor of A.F.A.*

Mr. Abel, I appreciate the opportunity to be in your classroom today. Your lesson directly supported our vision for literacy by implementing the discussion rounds for your students. It was terrific that Allan read the first excerpt, then had to wait until Simone and Luis responded to the two guiding questions: "What do they think it means? Why is it important?"

After they responded, you then circled back to Allan who had to explain their responses, as well as explain if he agreed or disagreed. This is a textbook student discourse strategy. The structure you created, balances who talks and also requires each student to use evidence-based reasoning. As you know, student discourse is a key priority within our literacy plan this year and I thank you for being so committed to mastering these strategies and reinforcing literacy in your classroom.

In this example, the teacher planned and executed a student discourse strategy. The feedback is Specific Praise for excellence, anchored to the vision and the key priorities. The observer even references the literacy plan as an aspect of the school's vision work. Anchoring to the vision isn't always about going directly back to the actual school vision, but can also anchor to other predefined key priorities.

▶ *Example #4: Specific Praise with an Emphasis on Align of A.F.A.*

Ms. Laughlin, I appreciate being in your classroom today. Thank you for using a Socratic seminar to reinforce our literacy initiative and for using a strategy that was taught in our last PD. It's awesome to see teachers implementing right after they learn something new. I realize that Socratic seminars require time to teach the students how to do it well, and I was wondering if this was the first time you used this strategy with this class? What steps have you taken to teach the students how to lead and interact in a Socratic seminar? I'm curious because it went so well today, and I want to be able to help others get to this level. Nicely done.

This final example reflects Specific Praise with the observer having a couple additional questions. This is perfectly natural during a walkthrough because there may be a variety of reasons for the teacher's actions, especially when learning a complex strategy like the use of Socratic seminars. This last example is about alignment to new professional development, and the leader is curious to learn more about the teacher's process to help even more teachers with effective use of the strategy. This helps to elevate teacher voice while aligning feedback to professional learning at the same time.

> **LEADER WELL-BEING SIDE NOTE: STAY CONSISTENT—BEWARE OF THE NOVELTY OF NEW**
>
> The lure of "new" attracts and deceives many leaders. This is a temptation that leaders have to be aware of and consciously resist. It's understandable how leaders fall victim to new because new feels exciting, it elicits energy, and can even provide a renewed sense of hope. New creates an illusion of progress because it's often equated wrongly with forward momentum.
>
> Leaders think, *If we're doing something new, we must be moving forward.* The truth, though, is the discipline of seeing efforts through, embracing the grind, and understanding real success through quick wins, is what creates sustained teacher growth and student achievement.
>
> Staying anchored in the vision, focused on incremental and consistent improvements, and aligning everything to PD is what succeeds in the end. Coherence isn't just good for the system, it's good for everyone's overall well-being and sanity. Burnout is real, and it's exasperated when efforts and initiatives are fragmented, dismissed too quickly, or allowed to pile up, creating overload and overwhelm. Stay the course and beware of the novelty of new.

▶ CONCLUSION

One of the major issues with schools today is that there is simply too much going on. The noise is deafening. We're not suggesting that all of these things aren't important; however, effective school leaders don't treat everything as having equal value. They realize that more noise creates more congestion and, often, in an already overcrowded system. A.F.A. serves as the filter that reduces the noise, which transforms the most aligned ideas into coherent action. The same understanding is necessary when providing feedback to teachers—less is more.

While Larisa was skilled at all three methods of quality feedback, she lacked a structure to keep her anchored, focused, and aligned. Yoda was proud of Larisa. She embodied the spirit of learning and willingness to improve that we want all educators possess. He reminded her that the power of A.F.A. is that it is not an abstract idea that is hard to grasp and implement. Rather, it is a practical framework that eliminates scattered ideas, disconnected actions, and random feedback by replacing it with clarity and coherence.

Larisa thought hard about A.F.A. as a transformational feedback tool that guides decisions, actions, and behaviors. By providing leaders with the structure to ensure their energy is focused and disciplined, the work is channeled in a way that continually drives student achievement. Ultimately, coherence is the antidote to fragmentation. It allows the vision, progress, and professional learning to carry the weight and meaning necessary to improve instruction and student outcomes.

When leaders act as the chief coherence navigators who intentionally anchor priorities, focus their energy on change, and align practices to action, they create the conditions for both teachers and students to thrive. A.F.A. is far more than a framework; it's a mindshift toward leading schools with coherence, clarity, and purpose.

▶ Next Steps Checklist

- Conduct an initiative audit to determine how clearly aligned your school initiatives are to your top priorities. As you identify fragmentation, decide if it can be eliminated. If it cannot, for whatever reason, regulate the time and attention it needs and stick to only giving it the energy it deserves.
- When using A.F.A. as your clear structure for feedback, ensure that you communicate the structure and rationale

to your staff. Coherence begins with everyone being on the same page, which means understanding a school leader's intentions and process for feedback.
- Use the A.F.A. model when providing feedback to teachers. While Specific Praise, Performance Coaching, and Professional Dialogue serve as the primary tactics of feedback, A.F.A. ensures that they are coherent.
- Be sure to check your feedback and discern how it corresponds with A.F.A.
- Monitor the impact that A.F.A. is making. Track how teachers are applying PD and your feedback in practice. Be sure to celebrate excellence and effort, identify gaps, and lean on A.F.A. to guide next steps.

Reference

Fullan, M., & Quinn, J. (2016). *Coherence: The right drivers in action for schools, districts, and systems.* Thousand Oaks, CA: Corwin (SAGE).

8 Dealing with Resistance

▶ **JAMAR'S TEACHERS ARE PUSHING BACK**

Jamar is a second-year principal at Smithfield, which is a choice school in Haverton County. He's been tasked with improving test scores to advance student achievement, which is reflected on the school, district, and state report card. One of his greatest challenges is that his teachers see very little value in the assessments, and they contend that there's misalignment between the tests, the curriculum, and overall relevance for "these students." Smithfield is a career and technical school (CTE) where students earn advanced credentials, which are not part of the accountability equation for the state. Every high school is held accountable to the same standards, which include SAT and ACT scores. The teachers, especially the CTE teachers, don't see value in scores that students would use to go to college because many of their students go directly into the workforce as apprentices after graduation.

Jamar thinks differently about the scores, though. He understands his teachers' rationale, but philosophically he believes in removing as many barriers as possible for students. He believes that the students should do well with their credentialing assessments and also have additional opportunities by scoring well on the SAT and ACT so they can pursue higher education whenever they choose to. He's working hard to help the teachers understand the overall benefits in improving the students' SAT and ACT scores, even underscoring the ever-changing landscape of career and technical education. Many of the programs they are bringing into the high school have career trajectories that require advanced degrees, such as becoming a Registered Nurse. One of his major strategies is to visit classrooms and provide feedback to teachers regarding their instructional strategies and student engagement, specifically with a focus on rigor. He wants high-quality instruction, backed by research, with a concentration on reading, writing, and computational skills. The school has a set of Principles of Instruction, and Jamar uses AFA to reinforce their use.

The problem is that even with solid Performance Coaching that he learned from Yoda his teachers aren't making the changes that he prescribes. Some of them have even noted to Jamar that they were at this school before he arrived and that they'll be here when he leaves. One teacher even visited Jamar's office with a coffee mug just to say that the mug was older than Jamar, and it's been his "school mug" since he started. To make matters worse, the district Director of Secondary Teaching and Learning recently stopped by to tell Jamar that she had no faith in the school or his turnaround efforts. "Good luck" she said, "This school has been a district project forever." Taken aback, Jamar responded, "Are you here today for a certain reason," "Yes," she replied, "To tell you good luck, but it ain't gonna happen, not with these teachers."

Fortunately, Jamar wasn't discouraged. He is a huge fan of Rita Pierson and lives by her words that "Every child deserves a champion, an adult who will never give up on them, who understands the power of connection, and insists that they become the best that they can possibly be" (Pierson, 2013). He believes in the teachers, he believes in the students, and he believes in himself. Plus, Yoda had one more trick up his sleeve. Yoda shared a framework that he uses as a tool when teachers are resistant. It never fails to get them to make the necessary changes to improve or to decide to work at another school with lower expectations for their performance and, unfortunately, their students. In those schools, there are also likely fewer classroom visits that the teachers have to "deal with." Yoda was clear that the framework was to be used to create clear lines of communication and motivate people, not get them to quit. However, critical dialogue can lead to expectations that some teachers decide to avoid before the consequences get too serious.

▶ YOUR PERFORMANCE COACHING CONVERSATIONS AREN'T CHANGING BEHAVIORS

Jamar has everything in place to move the needle. His system for visiting classrooms is working. The school has a set of Principles of Instruction, and he uses all three models of feedback effectively—Specific Praise, Performance Coaching, and Professional Dialogue. He even uses A.F.A. to anchor the vision, focus on incremental improvements, and align to professional development. Jamar is a very strong instructional leader, but his teachers are resistant to change, and, in a few cases, downright insubordinate. He doesn't want to threaten them with progressive discipline, nor does he feel that the teacher evaluation system should be used as a tool for dismissal. He truly desires to build a culture where teachers are motivated by student success and see the value in continuous improvement. Even though Jamar possesses almost every facet of a strong instructional leader, he's falling into three traps when his teachers are unwilling to change.

▶ *Trap #1: Being Unclear about the Core of the Problem*

The first trap when teachers are reluctant or resistant to change is being unclear about the core of the problem. Addressing what needs to change and explaining how to do it, even backed with a strong rationale, isn't enough for reluctant teachers because they don't believe that there's a problem that needs a resolution. In these cases, the leader knows what the problem is, but continues to use Performance Coaching, which works in most cases, but not when the person doesn't see the problem or any reason to change.

That's actually the biggest issue when coaching conversations aren't working—the divide between the observer and the teacher regarding the perceived problem. The teacher doesn't realize the gravity of the problem and the observer assumes they do. Until we explain the problem in detail and how it is detrimental, our Performance Coaching is limited to an expectation that the teacher will change behaviors because of our feedback. The truth is that resistant teachers aren't going to make changes simply because there's a coaching model in place or the observer gives them feedback. It's mostly likely that they're not interested in the feedback in the first place.

The first goal, when dealing with resistance, is to clearly define the problem. Even if the teacher still doesn't agree that there's a problem, they at least understand that you're naming a problem that *you* want them to fix. For example, you may want to see teachers cultivating student discourse as a powerful avenue to amplify student voice, but the teacher doesn't think student collaboration and communication are worthwhile. As a result, they would rather maintain control of student interactions and pacing through lecture. You can use all the Performance Coaching in the world and never see a change. But, if you name the problem—*we're focused on student discourse as one of our Principles of Instruction, and it's not observable in your classroom. I want that to change this week because, as a school, we are focused on deepening student learning, creating structures for all students to participate, and enabling them to speak effectively, which are all essential workplace and life skills.* This communication builds clarity around the difference between what the teacher understands as acceptable and what you identify as a problem.

▶ Trap #2: Struggling to Explain an Alternative

The second trap that leaders fall into when teachers are resisting a change is struggling to explain an alternative instructional strategy to use. Identifying the problem is only the start. Resistance doesn't necessarily mean defiance; it's sometimes due to a lack of skills or clarity about what to do differently. Non-resistant teachers often have other skill sets and confidence to search and find ways to do things differently on their own. Through Performance Coaching, you can ask them to make a change, and they'll do their best to find new ways to do things and try them out. By contrast, resistant people won't pursue alternatives for a number of reasons.

First, in the past, they've been told to do things differently, and no one followed up to check to see how well they were progressing. We'll come back to this in the third trap, but the lack of follow-through creates resistance. Second, change-resisters are almost always veteran teachers. Often, working for a number of administrators, good or bad, and they've come to live by the philosophy that *this too shall pass*. They're willing to sit back and do things the way they've always done them, believing that they will outlast or outwill you. Third, they've been teaching the same way for so long that they don't know how to change and aren't willing to do the work that it takes to change. Just telling them to change or identifying a problem won't motivate them to take action.

Part of the antidote for teachers in this category is to describe exactly what you want them to do differently and why. For example, if a teacher doesn't begin their lesson with a warm-up, and you want them to start every lesson with some type of activation strategy, just telling them to start the lesson with a warm-up next time isn't going to spark a change. Even when you describe how it's problematic for learners when they don't begin with established routines that actively pull the learner into the lesson. Explaining exactly what you want to see and why is a better approach. Take a look at the following language that could be used after the problem is identified.

For your next lesson, please post a warm-up on the board that requires students to recall and connect with yesterday's lesson. Use an open-ended question that doesn't have a single right answer, such as: What do you remember from yesterday's lesson that we might build on today?

▶ Trap #3: Failing to Follow Up on Expectations

As we mentioned in the second trap, the third trap is simply not following up on clearly established expectations and holding individuals accountable. Unfortunately, this is a common mistake for busy instructional leaders—failing to intentionally revisit the classroom to determine how well the suggested expectation is being executed. Of course, you'll revisit the classroom again, but not necessarily with the sole intent of seeing the warm-up. For example, we work with administrative teams all the time, training them to time-block their calendars to ensure that they visit every classroom in their school, every week. Let's imagine that you have your calendar blocked and the structures in place to conduct your visits. Even if you visit a classroom this week, don't see the warm-up, identify that as the problem, and clearly explain what to do differently, you might not be back next week at the beginning of the period when the warm-up should occur. Depending on your walkthrough rotation, you might not even be the next person to visit this particular teacher.

Your classroom visits, during the next week and the week after that, might not naturally be at the beginning of the period, which means that you aren't in a position to see how your recommendations are going. This means that the teacher is off the hook for months before you might be back at the beginning of the period, only to be frustrated that you're still not seeing the use of a warm-up. If you don't follow up on the specifics of your expectation, resistant teachers will wear you down every time. They've done it before, and they're well aware of how it works. You might even be back a month later, identify the problem again, explain the change, and repeat the cycle until the end of the school year, at which point the teacher got away with not changing their practice all year long.

Very often, when you ask a resistant teacher to change, there's work that they need to do that they're not used to doing or that they even know how to do. When you ask someone to make a change, and it means more work for them—thinking, preparing, planning—it also means that you have more work to do too. Following up the next week requires you to find a mutually agreed upon time to revisit at the beginning of the period and blocking that time to return. If you don't set up the next visit promptly to see the teacher implement the changes you requested, you've fallen into the trap. As the saying goes, what gets managed, gets done, which is why we emphasize organizing your calendar because it's one of the most important "time" strategies that you have.

▶ ELIMINATING THE OPTION TO RESIST

Your feedback, even informal feedback, as the school leader should not be perceived as something that is optional for the person to implement. Many educators have worked in environments where the leader's feedback was a suggestion, and especially in schools that aren't producing outcomes, that can no longer be the case. There are even evaluation and appraisal tools that position feedback as a "suggested" option. The narrative whereby the leader's feedback is simply a suggestion or that it can be debated and refuted is detrimental to progress.

This is especially true with resistant teachers. Your approach must be different with them given the fact that the circumstances are different. Working with resistant teachers demands a differentiated approach and the use of skills that are different from the ones we use with everyone else. If not, that would be like a doctor prescribing all of their patients the same dosage of high blood pressure medicine despite their particular blood pressure numbers. This one-size-fits-all approach is similar to continuing the use of Performance Coaching when it's not leading to changes in practice. In fact, if you're visiting every classroom, every week, you might find that some teachers need a new "dosage" of twice per week. Considering our example of the teacher who isn't using the prescribed warm-up strategy, you might adjust your calendar and let the teacher know that you're coming back the next day.

As the leader, you want to balance the complexity of the prescribed change that you're requiring the teacher to make with the realistic time that teachers will need, days or even weeks, to plan, prepare, and implement effectively. Sometimes the change is something that they need to observe another teacher doing so that they have a model and a clearer understanding of what it looks like in action. In that case, you'll need to give them time to schedule their observation before you come back to observe them. The intent is to eliminate their ability to resist by following up at a predetermined date and time.

If you allow the other aspects of leading a school to prevent you from returning in a timely manner and too much time goes by, you're setting yourself up for disappointment and frustration. In some cases, when a lot of time passes in between observations, the teacher might have tried the new strategy without you there, and it didn't work well. Not only did you fail to help the teacher make adjustments to it, you also reinforced the mindset that you weren't right about it being a better way to instruct students. Teachers who are open to feedback and change, will continue to iterate if this happens, but resistance teachers will dump the strategy and go back to their old ways. The only path forward is to follow up and be present when the change is scheduled to occur, which is why we developed our IDEAS framework.

▶ THE TIME: IDEAS

Our model for dealing with resistant teachers is called IDEAS, which is intentional because we still want there to be an exchange of thoughts—even with resistant people. If you're to the point where you need to tell someone exactly what to do rather than explaining an alternative strategy and letting them make some decisions about it, they probably already need an improvement plan of some sort. The IDEAS framework is designed to serve as a growth opportunity, so the teacher doesn't go directly on to an improvement plan. It's true that some teachers will require a documented plan and very specific instructions on what and how to change, but we like to start with a coaching framework that requires dialogue and discussion. We want teachers to learn and grow because they see the need to do so, not because their job is being threatened through a performance evaluation.

One thing to note about the model is that there are some variations to Part 4. Most of the time you're asking for a good time to follow up with them because the teacher has to make some decisions about when it's appropriate in their lessons and scope and sequence to use the new strategy. However, there are times when you need to just tell them when you'll be back. Imagine that your school has been working on warm-ups and activation strategies all year, it's one of your Principles of Instruction, you've done professional development at multiple faculty meetings, and your resistant teacher isn't using the strategy—and it's February. "I'll be back tomorrow" is a perfectly suitable response. Let's dive deeper into how the model works (Figure 8.1).

▶ *The Model*

The IDEAS framework has five parts to it, which are meant to be used in order, ending with you setting a date in your calendar to make a return visit. In the next section, you'll learn how each part works and why they're all important to combat resistance and initiate change as you lead the learning in your school. Parts 2 and 3 are similar to Performance Coaching but with more direction. Part 1 tells the teacher that there's a problem, which is slightly different than coaching people who are receptive to feedback. Parts 3 and 4 are the change makers that leaders often skip. Let's start with Part 1.

IDEAS

IDEAS equips school leaders to approach difficult conversations with clarity, care, and courage—creating a clear structure for change and a feedback culture built on trust and growth.

Figure 8.1 The IDEAS Framework

▶ Part 1: Identify the Core of the Problem

The first part of the IDEAS framework is to identify the problem without any ambiguity or interpretation so that leaders can focus the person on solving the right challenge. This is about facts, not feelings. Remember, you don't have to tell someone that they did something poorly to be able to explain a problem that needs to be fixed. In this case, you've already used Performance Coaching, and it's not working so we need to be crystal clear on the problem and that it's not okay to use the other less effective strategies. Candor is critical during this step.

If there's any doubt about what the exact problem is then the teacher is unlikely to change the behavior as you intended. If you're at this stage, you must conclude that resistant teachers don't know or agree that there's a problem, even if you've used Performance Coaching to guide them. You might say something like *today you called a student out from across the room, and I don't want you to do that again. Proximity to the student is vital and by calling out a student from across the room, you're more likely to escalate the situation than to manage their behavior.* Using another example, you might say, *today you used a popcorn reading strategy and there are far more effective strategies to use that we've learned at our faculty meetings.* The goal is to be ultra clear about exactly what the teacher did that is problematic and then move to Part 2 of the framework.

▶ *Part 2: Describe a Clear Alternative*

The next step is to describe a clear alternative. This is not a suggestion; you're telling the teacher what you want them to do differently in subsequent lessons. This type of authoritative directive is reserved for teachers who aren't changing fast enough to keep up with the school improvements that you're working to implement. That said, it requires you to be very clear about the strategies that you want teachers to use. Knowing that the teacher has participated in the professional learning and you've had Performance Coaching conversations on the strategies, but they're simply not changing.

In the case of the teacher who calls the student out from across the room, it wouldn't be sufficient to tell them to use a different strategy. They need to know that you want them to use proximity the next time the student doesn't follow directions. In the case of the popcorn reading strategies, you can't ask the teacher to use an alternative strategy without a clear description of a better option. In that case, you might say *next time please use the jigsaw strategy that we just reviewed on our recent professional development day*. For IDEAS to work, you need to be clear about the alternative method you want to see because you're going to return to see that exact strategy in action.

▶ *Part 3: Explain What It Looks Like in Action*

This next step is crucial because we can't assume that the teacher totally understands how to execute the new strategy even if they've received training. You're painting a picture of what the new desired behavior looks like in the classroom setting. This step is challenging for school leaders because we typically want to give them the benefit of the doubt, believing that they understand the power of proximity. But, in this case, you've already suggested the use of these strategies before, the teacher is familiar with them, and you explained why they're important—even describing what they can look like in action. The *why* behind the recommended alternative isn't relevant anymore or they would have done it. This is now a directive.

You'll say something like this: *when a student doesn't follow directions, please use proximity by walking over to the student's desk, kneeling down to their level, and asking them if they need help to get back on task.* In the case of the jigsaw not being used, you might even tell the teacher that they need to observe another teacher using the jigsaw method within the next few days. Explaining what it looks like in action might also include live or video observations, articles to read, or some type of "homework" that the teacher needs to complete. As an instructional leader, you've done the work to support this person, and they're not changing to meet the needs of the students. That means that they need to be put under more pressure to do so, which we'll come back to in the conclusion.

▶ Part 4: Ask for a Good Time to Follow Up

This is where we depart completely from Performance Coaching. Performance Coaching assumes that teachers will change on their own given proper feedback and the support to do so. IDEAS deviates from that assumption and initiates a new level of accountability through a follow-up. Performance Coaching does give the teachers the benefit of the doubt and rests on the teacher's professionalism that they will try the suggestion. The leader believes that when they return during their next walkthrough that the teacher will have used the feedback to make changes, either with effort (try something new even if it doesn't work well) or excellence (implement with accuracy and precision). By the time we are using IDEAS, we already know that this isn't the case.

You have two choices with the follow-up, and the first should be the most prevalent. The first choice requires you to ask the teacher for a time when she is going to use the strategy in the next week or so. Be clear that it should be within a week or two. You should base the timeline on how confident you are that the teacher can do what you're asking. If you think that they can plan, prepare, and execute without support, make it the following week. If you think they might need to see someone else do it first, make it two weeks from the visit. Do not go out any further than two weeks. The second choice lets the teacher know that you'll be back the next day or the next week to see the strategy in action. This only works in the case when it's a teaching strategy that should be used daily, such as objectives and criteria for success or a warm-up and closing activity.

▶ *Part 5: Schedule a Date to Return to Provide More Feedback*

The fifth part of the IDEAS framework takes us back to Chapter 2 with the importance of time-blocking. Do not leave the classroom without blocking the time to either revisit the teacher or to ensure that the teacher provides you with a time to return. Because you're most likely writing the feedback to the teacher (using the IDEAS framework) in an email or another walkthrough tracking system, and not directly talking to them, you'll need to collaborate with the teacher on a time to return or determine the best time to revisit on your own. Remember, there's no guarantee that the teacher will respond with a time so you should at least block the time to follow up with them if not the block of time to return.

There are times when you might have to physically visit the classroom to schedule a time to return or even tell the teacher, *I want you to plan to use a jigsaw strategy next Wednesday during your reading block so that I can make a return visit to observe the strategy in action and provide feedback on how well it unfolds.* Ideally, the teacher responds to your email with a date and time, which you'll need to time-block and protect at all costs. The two things that you do not want to happen is that the teacher uses the strategy without you there and it fails or you fail to show up on the date and time that they (or you) provided.

▶ **Examples**

▶ *Example #1: IDEAS that Aligns (A.F.A.) to Professional Development*

Mr. Landon, today, you used a round-robin reading strategy, which is an ineffective reading strategy that has the potential to negatively impact literacy skills. Next time you do a reading activity, please use the jigsaw strategy that we learned at our professional learning session. As we learned, break students into home groups, divide the reading into chunks, then let them go to their expert groups, read silently and then discuss as a group, pulling out the most important aspects of the reading. Then, have them go back to their home groups to "teach" their home partners. I know that you'll be doing more reading activities this week and next, please let me know a date and time that I can return within the next 10 days to observe you facilitating a jigsaw that I can provide feedback on.

The first two sentences cover Part 1 of the framework, which identifies the problem clearly. It may sound slightly harsh to call the teacher's selected strategy "ineffective," but remember, we're past the point of Performance Coaching, and we're trying to prevent a formal improvement plan, both of which mean that we need to be very candid and clearly express that the recommendation is non-negotiable. The third sentence indicates the alternative strategy, and the explanation for how to use it follows. In a Performance Coaching scenario, especially if the teacher participated in recent professional development on how to use the strategy, we might just ask the teacher to use the jigsaw; here, we need them to know the importance of the home and expert groups to support reading comprehension. The last sentence covers Part 4, and Part 5 occurs when we schedule ourselves to follow up to get the date and time, which is the most critical aspect of the framework.

▶ *Example #2: IDEAS that Aligns (A.F.A.) to Professional Development*

Mrs. Darling, today during my visit, you lectured for the entire 20 minutes I was present. Your students didn't have an opportunity to process or collaborate using the information on your slides. As we discussed at our recent professional learning series, the Ten + Two method provides ample opportunity for collaborative structures that are critical for students to translate the content into their own words, amplifying their voice and working to help them retain the material. There were several opportunities to do a simple think-pair-share (TPS) where you could have paused, given students a minute to think, had them turn to their shoulder partners, and discuss what they're learning. I want you to plan to use a simple TPS in the next few days (before the end of next week), and send me the date and approximate time that you plan to use it so that I can return to provide you with feedback. I look forward to seeing the TPS in action.

This is another example of the IDEAS framework combined with A.F.A. whereby the observer aligns the feedback to a recent professional learning experience. Plus, the professional learning is a "series," which means that the teacher has learned several strategies that are clearly not in place. There are a few things to note about the feedback beyond all five parts of the model being in place, which you can identify on your own. Note that the instructional leader is objective with what they saw: *you lectured the entire 20 minutes I was present.* Being objective and having data versus just sharing your opinion is important. A subjective and less effective statement could have been: *your students weren't engaged during the time I visited today.* This type of feedback is open to interpretation and invites disagreement and possibly an argument. That can be avoided through objectivity—the teacher lectured the whole time, and students didn't get a chance to discuss the material. We can't stress enough, though, that the leader has to schedule a time to ensure that the teacher sets the date for the return visit. Don't go more than 72 hours without either receiving the date and time or following up to get it.

▶ *Example #3: IDEAS that Focuses (A.F.A.)*
on the Vision (Principles of Instruction)

Mr. Fritz, today when I visited your classroom I observed a lesson that deviates completely from the new math curriculum. You were using materials and resources from the curriculum that we sunsetted last school year. Please do not use that curriculum anymore, and get back on track with the new curriculum, which includes the online and printed materials for both students and teachers. I want you to respond to this email with the date (no more than a few days after I send this) when you'll be back on track. I know that it may take another day or two to get through this unit, and I don't want you to abruptly stop, making it strange for the students, but in a few days, you'll need to be back on track, and I will visit then to ensure that you get feedback on the implementation of the new materials, resources, and strategies.

The difference with this example is that you might not have used Performance Coaching with Mr. Fritz in the past, but it's unacceptable for him to revert back to an old curriculum when a new one has been created or purchased and adopted. If there's a new vision for a mathematics curriculum, for example, and the teachers have been trained, they should not be using other resources and materials outside of the scope-and-sequence that's provided. In some cases, teachers have flexibility with this, but in the case of a school or district-wide adoption, teachers should not be using the old materials. Many teachers may use resources from sites like Teachers Pay Teachers, and, in cases where they don't have access to a research- and evidence-based curriculum that may be a last resort. But, in the case where they have what they need, it's the instructional leaders' job to ensure that they use it with confidence, fidelity, and precision. It's simply another reason why frequent visits with informal feedback are so important. The follow-up is essential because without it, Mr. Fritz might go on using the old curriculum for many more weeks, months, or even the rest of the school year.

▶ *Example #4: IDEAS that Focuses (A.F.A.) on the Vision (Principles of Instruction)*

Mrs. Wright, today I visited your classroom at the beginning of your reading block, and I didn't see a warm-up as an activation strategy. Not only is it important to start the period with routines, warm-ups are one of our Principles of Instruction that we expect teachers to use daily to start each period. I've noted that you skipped using a warm-up in the past when I visited your classroom at the beginning of a lesson, and it's my expectation that you use warm-ups as we've discussed. I'm going to return tomorrow at the start of one of your blocks; I expect to see a warm-up to begin the lesson, and I plan to provide feedback on how it goes.

This example deviates from asking the teacher to provide a date and time and moves to a model where you return the next day. It works for this example for several reasons. First, we've established the expectation that warm-ups are an essential aspect of every block of instruction, and warm-ups are one of our Principles of Instruction. Second, a warm-up is not something that the teacher needs time to plan, prepare, and place into a lesson at an intentional time for us to return to observe it.

Third, we've already had this conversation with the teacher, and she hasn't changed. It's fair and consistent to return the next day to see the warm-up in practice, and we might even move to a progressive discipline model, rather than an improvement plan, if it doesn't occur.

> **LEADER WELL-BEING SIDE NOTE: DEVELOP A TRIBE—BE SURE TO HAVE TRUSTED FRIENDS AND ADVISORS FOR MENTORSHIP AND SUPPORT**
>
> People are people, and even if your friends and advisors aren't educators, if they're leaders in any field, they have likely managed resistance as well. Whether it's someone to talk to for good advice or just a friendly "shoulder to cry on," you need people to call when you have a tough day. These should be people outside of your workplace relationships and, for the most part, not family members either. The reasons are many, but two important considerations are that you don't want to share sensitive information about people who may know the person you're talking about, and we don't want family to worry about our issues at work. Your tribe of advisors and mentors can be old friends, people you worked with in the past whereby one or both of you have moved on to new roles, or paid coaches as in the case of Yoda.
>
> For example, suppose you're not making progress with a teacher through Performance Coaching and you're anxious about being even more candid through the use of IDEAS. When you explain the resistance and push back, your tribe will help you with the confidence to move forward. Simple questions like, *Isn't it your job to ensure that students are engaged and learning?* Or, *Isn't it the role of the principal to improve teaching practices and outcomes for kids?* These conversations can act as drivers for motivation and action in the times when your self-talk isn't as positive as you want it to be.

▶ CONCLUSION

The IDEAS framework is not something you'll use with the majority of your teachers. In fact, in a normal productive environment, you'll use it with a small percentage. Even in a high needs turnaround school, it still might only be about 30 percent of the staff who resist change and need more than Performance Coaching to improve. The reason that it's important to understand is because there is almost always one or more teachers who are not responding to feedback to make changes to instruction to increase student engagement. Allowing these folks to continue on their personal path, ignoring the vision and goals of the school as a whole, will deteriorate the culture for everyone else.

We wrote about this in *Invest in Your Best* (Whitaker et al., 2023), a book for school leaders who want to elevate the work of their best teachers. The worst behavior, the worst instruction, and the worst attitude that you tolerate on your staff defines the culture of your school or district. When your average but steadfast teachers (we call them "backbones" in *Invest In Your Best*) and your best teachers know that there's a teacher down the hall who isn't implementing the *Principles of Instruction* or doesn't use the new curriculum, it gives everyone license to do as they please in one way or another. This erodes trust in the leader, eliminates coherence, and weakens any organization.

If you recall from the beginning of this chapter, Jamar, is a strong instructional leader who is skilled in all three tactics—Specific Praise, Performance Coaching, and Professional Dialogue, but if he doesn't confront and alter the resistant teachers' behaviors, attitudes, and actions using the IDEAS framework, he's going to continue to see modest student improvement. Worse yet, he will be frustrated and burned out. Charged with improving SAT and ACT scores, he needs to ensure that instruction—in every classroom, every day, and in every period—is preparing students for high levels of mathematics, reading and writing. But, if everyone isn't on board, he needs to use the IDEAS model to move the needle. When he begins to use IDEAS with the resistors, following up to revisit to observe what he expects and provide feedback, people change.

▶ Next Steps Checklist

- When teachers resist a change, be sure to identify the core of the problem with candor and clarity.
- When asking teachers to make a change to their practices, describe a clear alternative that you want them to implement.
- Explain what your alternative practice looks like in action so that the teacher understands exactly how they should execute the new strategy.

- Ask for a good time to return to observe the new practice or simply tell the teacher when you plan to revisit the classroom for additional feedback on the change.
- Make certain to schedule your next visit within days or weeks by blocking time so that your return without too much time passing while the status quo ensues.

References

Jones, J., & Vari, T. (2018). *Candid and compassionate feedback: Transforming everyday practice in schools.* New York: Routledge.

Pierson, R. (2013, May). *Every kid needs a champion* [Video]. TED Conferences.

Rosenshine, B. (2012). *Principles of instruction: Research-based strategies that all teachers should know.* Louisiana Department of Education. https://www.aft.org/sites/default/files/Rosenshine.pdf

Whitaker, T., Hamilton, C., Jones, J., & Vari, T. (2023). *Invest in your best: 9 strategies to grow, support, and celebrate your most valuable teachers.* Thousand Oaks, CA: Corwin.

9

Conclusion— Fostering Continuous Improvement

What you're building with these models for learning and lifting is called a *learning culture*. It's juxtaposed with a *teaching culture*. In a *teaching culture*, the environment doesn't expect nor support teachers to learn and grow. The emphasis is on compliance and standardization, not collaboration and continuous learning. In a *learning culture*, everyone in the school—the administration, the teachers, and the students—embrace a learner's mentality. Learning is the priority, which places the emphasis on growth, collaboration, and agency. Everyone comes to school—students and staff—to accept feedback, increase knowledge, improve skills, and get better. In this type of culture, the teachers aren't just trying to get better at teaching, they're focused on continual improvement, and, essentially, getting better at getting better. In this type of model, everyone feels the urgency and the pressure to improve. The key aspect of a learning culture, which is wholly the responsibility of the instructional leader, is providing the support necessary to meet the demands of the pressure to improve.

As the capstone to the time, tools, and tactics that we've reviewed thus far, we want to introduce the pressure and support "time" strategy that provides the infrastructure necessary for a culture that thrives feedback. Using the time, tools, and tactics appropriately requires leaders to set a standard of excellence that is reinforced through continual feedback. This can be counterintuitive for many school leaders in terms of how they view the pressure that's necessary for excellence. In *Candid and Compassionate Feedback* (2018) we introduced the concept of a "culture of nice" whereby leaders get trapped in believing that a positive school culture is where everyone is always trying to be nice to one another, even at the expense of results. We briefly mentioned it before, but this often stems from the desire for people to be happy at work. While being happy at work is a good thing, it doesn't come from lowering expectations, not holding people accountable, and hoping everyone does an excellent job. The reality is that great school cultures are built when people feel their work is purposeful, meaningful, and connected to a greater good. Happy workers are high achievers.

This requires leaders to set a high bar for teachers, clearly establish expectations, and intentionally support their growth. Done well, this approach energizes and motivates people in a way that makes them feel accomplished, resulting in satisfaction and a feeling of happiness about the work that they're doing and the purpose they serve. By using the time, tools, and tactics effectively, we break free from a "culture of nice" and enter into a space of integrity where people thrive within a cycle of continuous improvement. Think about it through the lens of health and wellness, when we exercise to lose weight and gain muscle, we don't see results right away. But, as we stay consistent by focusing on our goals, we begin to see and feel the change that we're seeking to make.

When that happens, we push ourselves even more, using the energy and motivation from the results. What's amazing is that our initial goals change after our success and we realize we can achieve so much more, so we alter what we're doing to make even greater gains. We tweak our diet, increase our workouts, and add different routines that we may have never thought possible. Pressure and support balance one another in a way that drives us to new heights and makes us feel good without experiencing stress and burnout.

As instructional leaders embrace this model, it's imperative to keep the exercise analogy top of mind. 1. It's all about the time you put into improving your fitness. Efficient use of time—both for rest and stress—are critical to recovery and growth. 2. Putting pressure on ourselves (working out) without proper support (equipment, rest, and diet) doesn't work. 3. All the support in the world (the best diet and rest) won't build muscle without time under pressure. These simple notions can be applied to school culture as well, but without the right balance, we won't see the results that we're working so hard to obtain. Let's dive deeper into the model.

▶ BALANCING PRESSURE AND SUPPORT

At the heart of the pressure and support model for continuous school improvement is balance. Pushing too far in one direction or the other can have dire consequences. There are times when it's necessary for pressure to be greater than support and vice versa, which lies in the leader's ability to accurately assess various situations. Well-informed instructional leaders who have a solid pulse on their teachers' strengths and weaknesses can determine what is needed at the right time. Great instructional leaders should always be thinking, *is it time for more pressure to improve or do the people need more support to make the changes associated with the vision?* Let's take a closer look at what happens when imbalance occurs.

In a situation where the leader applies *low pressure and low support* we end up with frustration and complacency. People get frustrated because things are getting better, and they become complacent by doing what they've always done without improved results. We typically see this result with laissez-faire leaders who want to maintain the status quo but who also don't know how to support people in their efforts or challenge those who are disengaged. The biggest problem with trying to maintain the status quo is that it will always result in diminished performance. In the low pressure, low support model, school systems experience rapid decline because there is little to no direction, guidance, and support. As a result, nothing changes and current conditions worsen.

The next scenario is the *low pressure, high support* model, which is also the most common, especially given the prevalence of a "culture of nice" in schools. This comes from a leader's desire to avoid disruption by "supporting" teachers in their current efforts, allowing them to do as they fit without establishing high standards and accountability measures. Leaders in this quadrant are "comfort seekers" or "peacekeepers," operating under the false belief that things will get better as long as they "support" their people. The decline in this case happens so gradually that it's often imperceptible, until the quiet disappointment sets in; despite all of the "support," nothing is truly getting better.

The third quadrant is one of *high pressure and low support*. When a culture suffers from this type of imbalance, people become stressed, fatigued, and worse yet, burned out. We find this situation in school systems where there is an enormous amount of outside pressure to improve that even the leader is stressed out and on the brink of burning out. This stress is passed on to the staff without the proper support, and it ultimately impacts the students. We might see a few fleeting gains within this model, due to the concentrated effort and focus, but they're typically temporary. With too much pressure in the system and not enough support to reach the goals, we end up with stagnation, frustration, burnout, and eroded performance. Given the choice, people will stay within the ineffectiveness of the low pressure, low support and the low pressure, high support model, but they'll leave quickly if there's too much pressure and not enough support.

The final model is the goldilocks of pressure and support: *high pressure, high support.* The interesting thing about the high pressure, high support model for continuous improvement is that you can drive significant pressure for change into the system as long as you balance it with an equal amount of support. This is why we see such rapid school improvement in this model because it garners the flywheel effect that comes from a series of consistent efforts that build toward significant breakthroughs. When people make small, supported changes incrementally, it leads to massive improvements over time. People are energized by this type of achievement and motivated to do even more because of the impact that they're having on the goal—which is always student achievement and well-being.

Q3: High Pressure, Low Support *Response:* Stress and Burnout *Result:* Unsustainable Gains with Intermittent School Improvement	**Q4: High Pressure, High Support** *Response:* Energy and Motivation *Result:* Rapid and Sustainable School Improvement
Q1: Low Pressure, Low Support *Response:* Frustration and Complacency *Result:* Status Quo with Rapid Decline	**Q2: Low Pressure, High Support** *Response:* Delusion and Disappointment *Result:* Comfort with Slow Decline

Q4 —high pressure, high support—leadership is rare, not because it's overly complex, but because it requires consistent courage and accountability. School leaders are often afraid of the consequences of high pressure, especially when they may not be experiencing the same degree of support themselves. It's easy to fall into Q1 and Q2 when the external demands for change are low, but great instructional leaders are always working toward excellence in the classroom—using Specific Praise, Performance Coaching, and Professional Dialogue. To be in Q4 requires balance and expertise and an understanding of what pressure and support look like in action as well as the time that one can spend on pressure and support to achieve balance.

▶ THE TIME: A PRESSURE AND SUPPORT MODEL

Applying pressure and support is all about the amount of time and effort you spend on each in comparison with the other and in unison with the needs of the school and the individuals who work within it. In other words, pressure and support drives a culture of continuous improvement and continuous improvement defines the culture. The instructional leader's job is to understand what pressure looks and feels like and which supports are necessary so that the pressure doesn't cause unnecessary, unhealthy, or unsupported stress. Let's look at a few examples.

> **Q4: High Pressure, High Support**
> *Response:* Energy and Motivation
> *Result:* Rapid and Sustainable School Improvement

Throughout this book, we used literacy examples—the use of reading strategies and the implementation of literacy across the curriculum to support our points of view. Imagine an instructional leader with this same vision for non-ELA classrooms, applying pressure on the teachers to use literacy strategies without offering quality professional development. This is an example of a high-pressure, low-support model. But, the more professional development that the teachers receive and the more examples within their curriculum that are developed, the more pressure can be applied through Performance Coaching and the IDEAS frameworks. The problem arises when we decide that literacy will be our schoolwide instructional initiative, and we don't properly train the teachers or develop measures of accountability to see how well teachers are developing and to what extent the initiative is progressing. The time spent on professional learning (PL) must be balanced with the instructional leader's time spent on classroom visits with feedback that employ the tactics—Specific Praise, Performance Coaching, Professional Dialogue, and, when necessary, IDEAS.

Throughout the book, we've also explored the concept of Principles of Instruction (PoI). To reiterate, Principles of Instruction are evidence-based instructional strategies that give teachers a clear roadmap for helping students learn more effectively. They emphasize small, intentional steps in instruction, frequent checks for understanding, and consistent opportunities for practice and feedback, all designed to boost retention and application (Rosenshine, 2012). Just having Principles of Instruction provides support because it gives clarity around the strategies that we want our teachers to use when planning.

But, leaders also need to make sure that they provide frequent and sustained professional learning opportunities so that teachers continue to learn and grow. Research suggests that meaningful impact often requires close to 50 hours of ongoing learning in a given area (Darling-Hammond et al., 2009; Darling-Hammond et al., 2017). Once we feel that our teachers have received the appropriate amount of PL and they've had time to apply their new skills, then we can provide Performance Coaching and continually add pressure for them to perform at a high level. Without PoI, or PL to support them, we fall right back into Q3, which we know leads to unsustainable gains with intermittent school improvement.

When we use all of the time, tools, and tactics referred to in this book fluidly with one another, the school environment changes for the better and the speed at which everyone improves increases dramatically. Imagine the following sequence of events: you communicate a vision to emphasize literacy with an enhanced focus on students' speaking and listening skills. This vision is supported through intentional classroom efforts to amplify student voice through structured collaboration; you provide a sequenced professional learning series on how to plan, prepare, and implement collaborative structures in every lesson; you visit classrooms frequently to provide feedback specifically on collaborative structures; you provide teachers with Specific Praise for their efforts and excellence with collaborative structures; and you add layers of strategies for collaboration to improve practice throughout the school year. Over time, incremental changes occur, leading to massive improvements in instruction and student voice. Everyone improves, data reveals this success, staff feels their impact, and students are learning at grade level. That's a culture of continuous improvement where you're leading learning as an instructional leader.

▶ A FINAL WORD ON SCHOOL IMPROVEMENT

A lot has been said and written about school improvement and the need for assistant principals and principals to be instructional leaders. We also know that clear supports and structures must be in place for them to know how to be effective instructional leaders within the school day. We've trained 1000s of school leaders at this point, and we consistently find assistant principals, principals, directors, and superintendents who are overwhelmed by the urgent work and fires that rage each day, resulting in missed opportunities to effectively lead and focus on the work that generates student success. We hope that this book provides clear time, tools, and tactics that support leaders to reclaim their time, reinvigorate their passion, and focus on the work that really changes the lives of our students.

As you've read, we have outlined the *time, tools, and tactics* to help instructional leaders improve their practice and focus on the highly effective efforts that make a real difference in our schools. When all of these strategies work together, they create coherence by having each piece fall into place so that the daily work of leadership aligns with the larger mission of improving teaching and learning. Leadership is never about managing disconnected tasks or the random urgent issues; it is about orchestrating the daily work of an administrator into a unified effort that drives continuous improvement.

And while being a school and district administrator can feel overwhelming, it certainly doesn't have to be done in isolation. We often say that the silos that teachers find themselves in are even more isolating for administrators. Every leader needs a mentor or guide, a trusted voice who can help them see more clearly, challenge their ideas, and remind them of their greater purpose. In our book, we've mentioned Yoda, the master coach. We are inspired by Yoda's role in the *Star Wars* saga, which was not to fight the battles for others, but to provide wisdom, encouragement, and clarity so that the hero could fulfill his potential. In the same way, great leaders seek mentors, coaches, and colleagues who help them navigate challenges, sustain their energy, and keep their vision alive.

Our hope is that the principles, practices, models, and perspectives we've shared throughout this book serve as both a compass and a toolkit. It is our greatest desire that you continue to grow in your leadership, build coherence in your schools, and remember that while the journey is yours, you don't have to go it alone. TheSchoolHouse302, the original concept designed by the authors, was built on the idea of collaboration, support, and growth during the era of No Child Left Behind. We hope that you experience the success we have, and, if this book changes your practice, then we hope that you'll share it with other school leaders who desperately want to be effective instructional leaders, but need the time, tools, or tactics to achieve their vision.

References

Darling-Hammond, L., Hyler, M. E., & Gardner, M. (2017). *Effective teacher professional development.* Learning Policy. https://learningpolicyinstitute.org/sites/default/files/product-files/Effective_Teacher_Professional_Development_REPORT.pdf

Darling-Hammond, L., Wei, R. C., Andree, A., Richardson, N., & Orphanos, S. (2009). Professional learning in the learning profession: A status report on teacher development in the United States and abroad. National Staff Development Council.

Rosenshine, B. (2012). *Principles of instruction: Research-based strategies that all teachers should know.* Louisiana Department of Education. https://www.aft.org/sites/default/files/Rosenshine.pdf